STEP-BY-STEP

50 Classic Curries

Manisha Kanani

Photography by David Jordan

AURA BOOKS

To my mother and grandmother – who have taught me everything I know.

First published in 1996 by Lorenz Books

This edition published in 1996 by Aura Books

© 1996 Anness Publishing Limited

Lorenz Books is an imprint of
Anness Publishing Limited
1 Boundary Row
London SE1 8HP

ISBN 1 85967 276 0

A CIP catalogue record is available from the British Library

Publisher: Joanna Lorenz
Senior Cookery Editor: Linda Fraser
In-house Editor: Anne Hildyard
Designer: Alan Marshall
Photographer: David Jordan
Food and props styling for photography: Judy Williams

Printed and bound in Hong Kong

AUTHOR'S ACKNOWLEDGEMENTS
I would like to thank Girish Bhogra, Ketan Natalia, Judy Williams, David Jordan
and Meena Unarket, all of whom have helped in their own special way.
Thank you for helping turn a dream into a reality. Above all, I would like to
thank my family (especially my mum) for their patience, support and
encouragement throughout the last few months, and for tasting my numerous
creations with such enthusiasm. I'm sure they've all had enough of curries
for a while.
Manisha Kanani

For all recipes, quantities are given in both metric and imperial
measures, and, where appropriate, measures are also given in standard
cups and spoons. Follow one set, but not a mixture, because they are
not interchangeable.

STEP-BY-STEP
50 Classic Curries

CONTENTS

Introduction	6
Basic Spice Mixes	16
Techniques	18
Dips and Relishes	20
MEAT DISHES	22
POULTRY DISHES	34
FISH AND SEAFOOD	50
VEGETABLE DISHES	60
RICE AND PULSES	80
Index	96

INTRODUCTION

The popularity of Indian food has continued to grow over the years and supermarkets are now selling a wide range of spices, vegetables and special ingredients. Cooking Indian food has never been easier.

There is a misconception that Indian food is time-consuming and difficult to cook. Nothing could be further from the truth. With a basic understanding of the spices and their influences, Indian cooking can be simple.

The secret of Indian cooking lies in the imaginative use of spices. Different cooking techniques bring out a different flavour from each spice. The combination of flavours and variety of tastes is endless. No other cuisine offers such a diverse spectrum of dishes.

There is no rigid structure to an Indian meal. All the dishes are served at once and everyone helps themselves. A meal should have a good balance of moist and dry dishes, and bread and rice are always served, accompanied by poppadums and a selection of pickles and chutneys.

You will find some well-known restaurant favourites in this book such as Chicken Tikka Masala and Mixed Vegetable Curry, together with some more innovative dishes, all of which illustrate the versatility of Indian cooking. There is nothing more satisfying about Indian food than when it is freshly cooked at home. If you always believed that long, slow cooking methods and complicated preparations were essential to create the authentic tastes and aromas of Indian food then this book will prove to be a refreshing culinary experience – and allow you to enjoy cooking and eating in true Indian style.

Spices

It is the blending of spices, seasonings and flavourings that gives Indian food its character.

Bay leaves
These fragrant leaves are used in many meat and rice dishes (1).

Cardamom
These pods are green, black and creamy-beige, green being the most common. Whole pods used in rice and meat dishes to add flavour should not be eaten. Use black seeds in desserts (2).

Chilli powder
The strength of this powder varies, depending on the chilli. It is very hot and used often (3).

Cinnamon
Cinnamon is available whole or ground. The sticks are used for flavour and are not eaten (4).

Cloves
Cloves are used in spice mixtures such as garam masala and in meat and rice dishes (5).

Coriander
One of the most popular spices, these small beige seeds are used whole and ground, giving a slightly sweet flavour. Coriander leaves are used for flavouring and as a garnish (6).

Cumin
Available as whole dark brown seeds and ground. The whole seeds are often fried in oil, releasing a strong musky flavour and aroma (7).

Curry leaves
These aromatic leaves are the Indian version of bay leaves (8).

Curry powder
There are many variations of this spice mixture, varying in both flavour and colour (9).

Dried chillies
These red chillies are often fried in oil to release their strong flavour. The small ones are the most pungent (10).

Fennel seeds
A small light green seed, similar in smell and taste to aniseed. They are used in many vegetable and meat dishes. Roasted fennel seeds are also eaten after a meal to freshen the mouth (11).

Fenugreek seeds
These small pungent seeds are used in spice mixtures (12).

Garam masala
This is the main spice mixture of Indian cooking. It is a hot and aromatic powder and is added at the end of cooking (13).

Garlic
Available fresh and dried, garlic is used for its strong flavour. The powder is mainly used in spice mixtures (14).

Ginger
Both fresh and ground ginger have a sharp refreshing flavour. Fresh root ginger should be peeled before use (15).

Mint
Fresh mint has a very refreshing flavour and is used for making chutneys and raitas (16).

Mustard seeds
Whole black mustard seeds are added to hot oil to release a nutty flavour. They are used with vegetables and pulses (17).

Nutmeg
Whole and ground, nutmeg has a sweet, nutty flavour (18).

Paprika
A mild, sweet red powder, paprika adds colour (19).

Peppercorns
Black peppercorns are used whole and ground. They are also used in garam masala (20).

Saffron
Saffron is the dried stigmas of the saffron crocus. It is used in savoury and sweet dishes for its aroma and colour (21).

Sesame seeds
Small and creamy-white with a rich, nutty flavour, these seeds are used in vegetable dishes and sprinkled as a garnish (22).

Tamarind
The tamarind pod is dried to form a dark brown, sticky pulp which is soaked in hot water, then strained before use. It has a strong, sour taste and is used in curries and chutneys (23).

Turmeric
Turmeric is a bright yellow powder and is primarily used for its colouring properties. Because of its strong, bitter flavour it should be used sparingly (24).

Vegetables

Indian cooking specializes in a hundred different ways of using vegetables, everything from cauliflower, potatoes and peas to the more exotic and unusual varieties of vegetables such as okra, bitter gourds and aubergines. When it comes to Indian cooking, vegetables are indispensable.

Aubergines
Available in different varieties, the shiny deep purple aubergine is the most common and widely used variety in Indian cooking. Aubergines have a strong flavour with a slightly bitter taste and are sometimes sprinkled with salt to extract some of these bitter juices (1).

Bitter gourds
One of the many very bitter vegetables often used in Indian cooking. This long, knobbly green vegetable comes from Kenya and has a strong, bitter taste. To prepare a gourd, peel the ridged skin with a sharp knife, scrape away and discard the seeds and chop the flesh (2).

Cauliflower
A large round vegetable with creamy white flowers and green leaves. This versatile vegetable is very popular in Indian cooking and is often combined with other vegetables (3).

Chillies
Chillies are small hot members of the capsicum family. There are many types, varying in shape, size, colour and flavour. Some are hotter than others. They are used extensively in Indian cooking, particularly the fresh green chilli. For a milder flavour, remove seeds before using (4).

Okra
Also known as ladies' fingers, okra is one of the most popular Indian vegetables. These small green five-sided pods have a very distinctive flavour and a sticky, pulpy texture when cooked (5).

Onions
A popular root vegetable belonging to the allium family, onions have a strong pungent flavour and aroma. Globe onions are the most commonly used variety for Indian cooking. Spring onions are also used in some dishes to add colour and for their mild taste (6).

Peppers
Peppers are large hollow pods belonging to the capsicum family and are available in a variety of colours. Red peppers are slightly sweeter than green peppers. They are used in a variety of Indian dishes, adding colour and flavour (7).

Spinach
Available all year round this green leafy vegetable has a mild delicate flavour. The leaves do vary in size but only the large thick leaves need to be trimmed of their stalks. Spinach is a popular vegetable in Indian cooking where it is cooked in many ways, both with meat and other vegetables (8).

Sweetcorn
Sweetcorn originated in America but is now grown all over the world. It has a delicious sweet, juicy flavour which is at its best just after picking (9).

Tomatoes
Tomatoes are available all year round in a variety of colours ranging from red to orange, yellow to green. They are an essential ingredient in Indian cooking and are widely used to make all sorts of sauces, chutneys and relishes (10).

Pulses, Lentils and Rice

Pulses and lentils play an important role in Indian cooking and are a good source of protein. Some are cooked whole, some are puréed and made into soups or "dhals" and some are combined with vegetables or meat. Rice is always served as part of an Indian meal.

Black-eyed beans
Sometimes called black-eyed peas, these small cream-coloured beans have a black spot or "eye". When cooked they have a tender, creamy texture and a mildly smoky flavour. Black-eyed beans are widely used in Indian cooking (1).

Chick-peas
These round beige-coloured pulses have a strong, nutty flavour when cooked. As well as being used for curries, chick-peas are also ground into a flour which is widely used in many Indian dishes such as pakoras and bhajees (2).

Chana dhal

Chana dhal is very similar to yellow split peas but smaller in size and with a slightly sweeter taste. It is used in a variety of vegetable dishes and can also be deep-fried and mixed with Indian crisps and spices such as in Bombay mix (3).

Flageolet beans

Small oval beans which are either white or pale green in colour. They have a very mild, refreshing flavour (4).

Green lentils

Also known as continental lentils, these have quite a strong flavour and retain their shape during cooking. They are very versatile and are used in a number of dishes (5).

Haricot beans

Small, white oval beans which come in different varieties. Haricot beans are ideal for Indian cooking because not only do they retain their shape but they also absorb the flavours of the spices (6).

Kidney beans

Kidney beans are one of the most popular pulses used in Indian cooking. They are dark red-brown, kidney-shaped beans with a strong flavour (7).

Mung beans

These are small, round green beans with a slightly sweet flavour and creamy texture. When sprouted they produce the familiar beansprouts. Split mung beans are also used in Indian cooking and often cooked with rice to make a popular Gujarati dish (8).

Rice

An annual cereal grass with many varieties. Different types of rice produce a different texture when cooked. Basmati rice is the most popular type eaten with Indian food. The long, slender grains have a distinctive and aromatic flavour (9).

Wash all varieties of rice in several changes of water and leave to soak before cooking. Rice can be cooked either by the absorption method, whereby the rice is cooked in a measured amount of liquid or, by the boiling method in which the rice is cooked in plenty of boiling water and then drained.

Toovar dhal

A dull orange-coloured split pea with a very distinctive earthy flavour. Toovar dhal is available plain and in an oily variety (10).

Red split lentils

A readily available lentil that can be used for making dhal. Use instead of toovar dhal (11).

SOAKING AND COOKING TIPS

Most dried pulses, except lentils, need to be soaked overnight before cooking. Wash the beans thoroughly and remove any small stones and damaged beans. Put into a large bowl and cover with plenty of cold water. When cooking, allow double the volume of water to beans and boil for 10 minutes. This initial boiling period is essential to remove any harmful toxins. Drain, rinse and cook in fresh water. The cooking time for all pulses varies depending on the type and their freshness. Pulses can be cooked in a pressure cooker to save time. Lentils, on the whole, do not need soaking. They should be washed in several changes of cold water before being cooked.

Breads

Breads are an integral part of any Indian meal. Most traditional Indian breads are unleavened, that is they do not contain any raising agent, and are made with ground wholemeal flour, known as chappati flour or *ata*. Some are dry-cooked on a griddle, some are fried with a little oil, others are deep-fried to make small savoury puffs. To enjoy Indian breads at their best they should be made just before a meal and eaten hot.

Chappati
This is the staple bread of northern and central India. Chappatis or *rotis* are very thin, flat, unleavened bread made from ground wholemeal flour. They are cooked on a hot *tava*, which is a concave-shaped Indian griddle. Chappatis have a light texture, are fairly bland in taste, but spices added with the flour give more flavour (1).

Naan
Naan is probably the most popular of all Indian breads. This large tear-shaped bread is traditionally cooked in a tandoor oven. They are normally made with plain flour enriched with yogurt and yeast, and can be eaten with most meat or vegetable dishes. There are many varieties of naan bread: plain naan, coriander and garlic naan, and masala naan (2).

Paratha
A paratha is similar to the chappati except that it contains ghee (clarified butter), which gives the bread a flaky texture. They are much thicker then chappatis and are shallow fried as opposed to dry-cooked. Plain parathas are often eaten for lunch and go well with most vegetable dishes. Parathas can also be stuffed with various fillings, the most popular being spiced potato, and are generally served on their own (3).

Puri
Also known as "poori", this is a small deep-fried puffy bread made from ground wholemeal flour. Puris are best eaten hot and are traditionally served for breakfast. They can be simply plain or flavoured with spices such as cumin, turmeric and chilli powder which are mixed into the dough. When served with a vegetable or fish curry, they make a perfect light snack or starter (4).

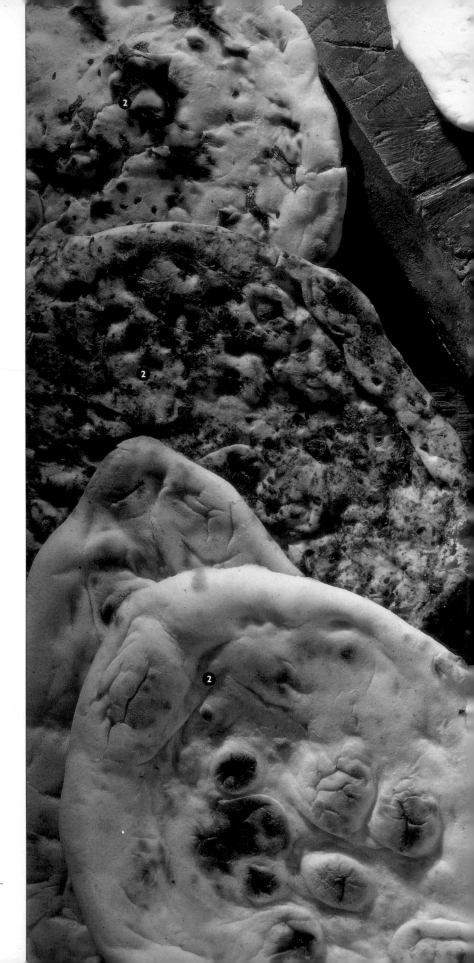

Basic Spice Mixes

Curry Powder

Curry powders do not exist in India. Most traditional Indian households use individual spices which are freshly ground and mixed, as and when they are needed. There are many commercially blended curry powders available but it is just as easy to make your own. This is a basic recipe for a mild curry powder but you can adjust the quantities to suit your taste.

Makes about 115 g/4 oz

INGREDIENTS
WHOLE SPICES
50 g/2 oz/¹/₂ cup coriander seeds
60 ml/4 tbsp cumin seeds
30 ml/2 tbsp fennel seeds
30 ml/2 tbsp fenugreek seeds
4 dried red chillies
5 curry leaves

GROUND SPICES
15 ml/1 tbsp chilli powder
15 ml/1 tbsp turmeric
2.5 ml/¹/₂ tsp salt

1 Dry-roast the whole spices in a large heavy-based frying pan for 8–10 minutes, shaking the pan from side to side until the spices begin to darken and release a rich aroma. Allow them to cool slightly.

2 Put the spices in a coffee grinder and grind to a fine powder.

COOK'S TIP
If you would like a hot curry powder then increase the quantity of dried red chillies.

3 Add the remaining ground spices and store in an airtight jar.

Garam Masala

Garam means "hot" and masala means "spices" so the spices used are those which "heat" the body, such as black peppercorns, cinnamon and cloves. Garam masala is added at the end of cooking and sprinkled over dishes as a garnish.

Makes about 50 g/2 oz

INGREDIENTS
10 dried red chillies
3 x 2.5 cm/1 in cinnamon sticks
2 curry leaves
30 ml/2 tbsp coriander seeds
30 ml/2 tbsp cumin seeds
5 ml/1 tsp black peppercorns
5 ml/1 tsp cloves
5 ml/1 tsp fenugreek seeds
5 ml/1 tsp black mustard seeds
1.5 ml/¹/₄ tsp chilli powder

1 Dry-roast the chillies, cinnamon sticks and curry leaves in a large heavy-based frying pan for 2 minutes.

2 Add the coriander and cumin seeds, peppercorns, cloves, fenugreek and mustard seeds and dry-roast for a further 8–10 minutes, shaking the pan from side to side until the spices begin to darken and release a rich aroma.

COOK'S TIP
The curry powder and garam masala will keep for 2–4 months in an airtight container. As with all spice mixes, the flavours will mature during storage.

3 Allow the mixture to cool slightly before grinding, then put the spices into a coffee grinder or use a pestle and mortar and grind to a fine powder. Add the chilli powder, mix together and store the powder in an airtight jar.

Curry Paste

A curry paste is a "wet" blend of spices cooked with oil and vinegar which help to preserve the spices. It is a quick and convenient way of adding a mixture of spices.

Makes about 600 ml/1 pint/2¹/₂ cups

INGREDIENTS
50 g/2 oz/¹/₂ cup coriander seeds
60 ml/4 tbsp cumin seeds
30 ml/2 tbsp fennel seeds
30 ml/2 tbsp fenugreek seeds
4 dried red chillies
5 curry leaves
15 ml/1 tbsp chilli powder
15 ml/1 tbsp turmeric
150 ml/¹/₄ pint/²/₃ cup white
    wine vinegar
250 ml/8 fl oz/1 cup oil

COOK'S TIP

Once the paste has been cooked, heat a little more oil and pour on top of the paste in the jar. This will help to preserve the paste and prevent any mould from forming.

1 Put all the whole spices into a coffee grinder or pestle and mortar and grind to a fine powder. Spoon into a bowl and add the remaining ground spices.

2 Mix all the ground spices with the vinegar and add 75 ml/5 tbsp water to form a thin paste.

3 Heat the oil in a large heavy-based frying pan and stir-fry the spice paste for 10 minutes or until all the water has been absorbed. When the oil rises to the surface the paste is cooked. Allow to cool slightly before spooning into sterilized jars.

Tikka Paste

A delicious, versatile paste which can be used in a variety of dishes such as Chicken Tikka Masala. This is a spicy paste with a slightly sour flavour.

Makes about 475 ml/16 fl oz/2 cups

INGREDIENTS
30 ml/2 tbsp coriander seeds
30 ml/2 tbsp cumin seeds
25 ml/1¹/₂ tbsp garlic powder
30 ml/2 tbsp paprika
15 ml/1 tbsp garam masala
15 ml/1 tbsp ground ginger
10 ml/2 tsp chilli powder
2.5 ml/¹/₂ tsp turmeric
15 ml/1 tbsp dried mint
1.5 ml/¹/₄ tsp salt
5 ml/1 tsp lemon juice
a few drops of red food colouring
a few drops of yellow
    food colouring
150 ml/¹/₄ pint/²/₃ cup white
    wine vinegar
150 ml/¹/₄ pint/²/₃ cup oil

1 Put the coriander and cumin seeds into a coffee grinder or use a pestle and mortar and grind to a fine powder. Spoon the spice mixture into a bowl and add the ground spices, mint and salt, stirring well.

2 Mix the spice powder with the lemon juice, food colourings and vinegar and add 30 ml/2 tbsp water to form a thin paste.

3 Heat the oil in a large heavy-based frying pan and stir-fry the paste for 10 minutes or until all the water has been absorbed. When the oil rises to the surface the paste is cooked. Allow the paste to cool slightly before spooning into sterilized jars.

TECHNIQUES

Skinning and Chopping Tomatoes

This is a very simple and easy way of preparing tomatoes for cooking and relishes.

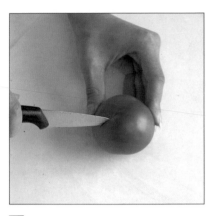

1 Using a small sharp knife, cut a small cross on the bottom of each tomato.

2 Put the tomatoes in a bowl and pour over boiling water. Leave for 20–30 seconds until the skin splits. Drain and transfer to a bowl of cold water.

3 Peel off the skin and chop finely.

Seeding and Chopping Chillies

Try using a fork and knife when preparing chillies to prevent your hands from burning.

1 Trim the chillies at both ends.

2 Cut the chillies in half lengthways.

COOK'S TIP
If you have sensitive skin wear a pair of rubber gloves.

3 Scrape away and discard the seeds using the tip of the knife and finely chop the flesh of the chillies.

Chopping Onions

A quick and easy way of cutting onions.

1 Cut the onion in half leaving the root intact and peel off the outer skin.

2 Place the cut side down and make horizontal cuts at 5 mm/¹/₄ in intervals making sure not to cut through the root.

3 Make vertical cuts in the same way at 5 mm/¹/₄ in intervals.

4 Hold the onion firmly with one hand and carefully chop finely.

Preparing Fresh Ginger

Fresh root ginger is very simple to prepare.

1 Break off a small piece of root ginger and remove any rough ends.

2 Peel off the tough skin using a small sharp knife or potato peeler.

3 Cut the ginger into thin slices and chop finely.

COOK'S TIP

Alternatively you can make ginger purée in a food processor or blender and freeze it in ice-cube trays. Once frozen, seal in a plastic bag. The purée will keep in the freezer for up to 2 months.

DIPS AND RELISHES

Cucumber Raita

A cool, refreshing relish, ideal with curries or served as a dip with dishes such as kebabs.

Makes about 600 ml/1 pint/2¹/₂ cups

INGREDIENTS
¹/₂ cucumber
1 green chilli, seeded and
 finely chopped
300 ml/¹/₂ pint/1¹/₄ cups
 natural yogurt
1.5 ml/¹/₄ tsp salt
1.5 ml/¹/₄ tsp ground cumin

1 Dice the cucumber finely and place in a bowl. Add the chilli.

2 Beat the yogurt with a fork until smooth and stir into the cucumber and chilli mixture.

3 Stir in the salt and cumin. Cover and chill before serving.

VARIATION
Instead of cucumber, use two skinned, seeded and chopped tomatoes and 15 ml/1 tbsp chopped fresh coriander.

Tomato and Chilli Chutney

If you like hot food then this spicy tomato chutney is the perfect accompaniment.

Makes about 475 ml/16 fl oz/2 cups

INGREDIENTS
4 tomatoes
1 red pepper
2 green chillies, roughly chopped
1 garlic clove, roughly chopped
1.5 ml/¹/₄ tsp salt
2.5 ml/¹/₂ tsp sugar
5 ml/1 tsp chilli powder
45 ml/3 tbsp tomato purée
15 ml/1 tbsp chopped
 fresh coriander

1 Roughly chop the tomatoes.

2 Halve the red pepper and remove the core and seeds. Roughly chop the red pepper halves.

3 Put all the ingredients into a food processor or blender together with 30 ml/2 tbsp water and process until fairly smooth. Cover and chill.

Coriander Chutney

A popular Indian side dish, this delicious chutney is made using fresh coriander.

Makes about 475 ml/16 fl oz/2 cups

INGREDIENTS
115 g/4 oz fresh coriander leaves
1 green chilli
2 garlic cloves, roughly chopped
5 ml/1 tsp salt
2.5 ml/½ tsp sugar
25 ml/1½ tbsp lemon juice
45 ml/3 tbsp ground peanuts

1 Roughly chop the coriander leaves.

2 Seed and roughly chop the chilli

3 Put all the ingredients into a food processor or blender together with 120 ml/4 fl oz/½ cup water and process until smooth. Cover and chill.

Mint and Coconut Chutney

This mild chutney has a delicious strong flavour.

Makes about 350 ml/12 fl oz/1½ cups

INGREDIENTS
50 g/2 oz fresh mint leaves
90 ml/6 tbsp desiccated coconut
15 ml/1 tbsp sesame seeds
1.5 ml/¼ tsp salt
175 ml/6 fl oz/¾ cup natural yogurt

COOK'S TIP

This chutney can be made in advance and will keep for up to five days in the fridge.

1 Finely chop the mint.

2 Put all the ingredients into a food processor or blender and process until smooth. Cover and chill.

Rogan Josh

The most popular dishes of all lamb dishes, the lamb is traditionally marinated in yogurt then cooked with spices and tomatoes which gives the dish its rich, red appearance.

Serves 4

INGREDIENTS
900 g/2 lb lamb fillet
45 ml/3 tbsp lemon juice
250 ml/8 fl oz/1 cup natural yogurt
5 ml/1 tsp salt
2 garlic cloves, crushed
2.5 cm/1 in piece root ginger, grated
60 ml/4 tbsp oil
2.5 ml/¹/₂ tsp cumin seeds
2 bay leaves
4 green cardamom pods
1 onion, finely chopped
10 ml/2 tsp ground coriander
10 ml/2 tsp ground cumin
5 ml/1 tsp chilli powder
400 g/14 oz can chopped tomatoes
30 ml/2 tbsp tomato purée
toasted cumin seeds and bay leaves,
    to garnish
plain rice, to serve

water

onion

chopped
tomatoes   oil

tomato
purée

garlic   ground
cumin

natural
yogurt

lemon
juice

ground
coriander

chilli
powder

lamb
fillet

salt   cumin
seeds

root ginger   cardamom pods

bay
leaves

1 Trim away any excess fat from the meat and cut into 2.5 cm/1 in cubes.

2 In a bowl, mix together the lemon juice, yogurt, salt, 1 garlic clove and the ginger. Add the lamb and leave in the marinade overnight.

3 Heat the oil in a large frying pan and fry the cumin seeds for 2 minutes or until they begin to splutter. Add the bay leaves and cardamom pods and fry for a further 2 minutes.

4 Add the onion and remaining garlic and fry for 5 minutes. Stir in the ground coriander, cumin and chilli powder and fry for 2 minutes.

5 Add the marinated lamb and cook for 5 minutes, stirring occasionally.

6 Add the tomatoes, tomato purée and 150 ml/¹/₄ pint/²/₃ cup water. Bring to the boil then reduce the heat. Cover and simmer for about 1–1¹/₂ hours or until the meat is tender. Serve with plain rice and garnish with toasted cumin seeds and bay leaves.

Matar Keema

One of the simplest Indian dishes to make. This spicy lamb curry can also be used as a tasty filling for stuffing vegetables such as peppers and large beefsteak tomatoes.

Serves 4

INGREDIENTS

45 ml/3 tbsp oil
1 onion, finely chopped
2 garlic cloves, crushed
2.5 cm/1 in piece root ginger, grated
2 green chillies, finely chopped
675 g/1½ lb minced lamb
5 ml/1 tsp ground cumin
5 ml/1 tsp ground coriander
5 ml/1 tsp chilli powder
5 ml/1 tsp salt
175 g/6 oz frozen peas, thawed
30 ml/2 tbsp lemon juice
naan bread and natural yogurt,
    to serve

chilli powder

ground cumin

peas

oil

lemon juice

garlic

minced lamb

green chillies

ground coriander

root ginger

salt

onion

1 Heat the oil in a large saucepan and fry the onion for 5 minutes until golden brown. Add the garlic, ginger and chillies and fry for 2–3 minutes.

2 Add the minced lamb and stir-fry for about 5 minutes.

3 Stir in the cumin, coriander, chilli powder and salt with 300 ml/½ pint/1¼ cups water. Cover and simmer for about 25 minutes.

4 Add the peas and lemon juice. Cook for a further 10 minutes, uncovered, or until the meat is tender. Serve with naan bread and natural yogurt.

Lamb with Apricots

Lamb is combined with apricots and traditional Indian spices to produce a rich, spicy curry with a hint of sweetness.

Serves 4

INGREDIENTS
900 g/2 lb stewing lamb
30 ml/2 tbsp oil
2.5 cm/1 in cinnamon stick
4 green cardamom pods
1 onion, chopped
15 ml/1 tbsp curry paste
5 ml/1 tsp ground cumin
5 ml/1 tsp ground coriander
1.5 ml/¼ tsp salt
175 g/6 oz ready-to-eat dried apricots
350 ml/12 fl oz/1½ cups lamb stock
yellow rice and mango chutney, to serve
fresh coriander, to garnish

lamb stock

ground cumin

onion

curry paste

oil

dried apricots

stewing lamb

salt

ground coriander

cardamom pods

cinnamon stick

1 Remove any visible fat and cut the meat into 2.5 cm/1 in cubes.

2 Heat the oil in a large saucepan and fry the cinnamon stick and cardamoms for 2 minutes. Add the onion and fry for about 6–8 minutes.

3 Add the curry paste and fry for 2 minutes. Stir in the cumin, coriander and salt and fry for 2–3 minutes.

4 Add the meat, apricots and the stock. Cover and cook for 1–1½ hours. Serve on yellow rice with the chutney in a separate bowl. Garnish with coriander.

Beef Madras

Madras curries originate from southern India and are aromatic, robust and pungent in flavour. This recipe uses beef but you can replace this with lamb if you prefer.

Serves 4

INGREDIENTS
900 g/2 lb stewing beef
45 ml/3 tbsp oil
1 large onion, finely chopped
4 cloves
4 green cardamom pods
2 green chillies, finely chopped
2.5 cm/1 in piece root ginger,
    finely chopped
2 garlic cloves, crushed
2 dried red chillies
15 ml/1 tbsp curry paste
10 ml/2 tsp ground coriander
5 ml/1 tsp ground cumin
2.5 ml/½ tsp salt
150 ml/¼ pint/⅔ cup beef stock
tomato rice, to serve
fresh coriander sprigs, to garnish

garlic   *root ginger*   *onion*

beef stock   *curry paste*   *stewing beef*

oil   *ground cumin*

ground coriander   *salt*   *cloves*   *cardamom pods*   *red chillies*   *green chillies*

1 Remove any visible fat and cut the meat into 2.5 cm/1 in cubes.

2 Heat the oil in a large frying pan and fry the onion, cloves and cardamom pods for 5 minutes. Add the fresh green chillies, ginger, garlic and dried chillies and fry for a further 2 minutes.

3 Add the curry paste and fry for about 2 minutes. Add the beef and fry for 5–8 minutes until all the meat pieces are lightly browned.

4 Add the coriander, cumin, salt and stock. Cover and simmer gently for 1–1½ hours or until the meat is tender. Serve with tomato rice and garnish with coriander sprigs.

Lamb Meatballs

Aromatic spices are combined with minced meat to produce authentic Indian-style meatballs.

Serves 4

INGREDIENTS

FOR THE MEATBALLS
675 g/1½ lb minced lamb
1 green chilli, roughly chopped
1 garlic clove, chopped
2.5 cm/1 in root ginger, chopped
1.5 ml/¼ tsp garam masala
1.5 ml/¼ tsp salt
45 ml/3 tbsp chopped fresh
    coriander

FOR THE SAUCE
30 ml/2 tbsp oil
2.5 ml/½ tsp cumin seeds
1 onion, chopped
1 garlic clove, chopped
2.5 cm/1 in root ginger,
    finely chopped
5 ml/1 tsp ground cumin
5 ml/1 tsp ground coriander
2.5 ml/½ tsp salt
2.5 ml/½ tsp chilli powder
15 ml/1 tbsp tomato purée
400 g/14 oz can chopped tomatoes
coriander rice, to serve
fresh coriander sprigs, to garnish

chopped tomatoes *green chilli* *chilli powder* *garlic* *root ginger* *tomato purée* *oil* *ground coriander* *garam masala* *ground cumin* *cumin seeds* *onion* *minced lamb* *fresh coriander*

1 To make the meatballs, put all the ingredients into a food processor or blender and process until the mixture binds together.

2 Shape the mixture into 16 balls. Cover and chill for 10 minutes.

3 To make the sauce, heat the oil and fry the cumin seeds until they splutter. Add the onion, garlic and ginger and fry for 5 minutes. Stir in the remaining sauce ingredients and simmer for 5 minutes.

COOK'S TIP
You can make the meatballs the day before. Cover with clear film and store in the fridge until needed.

4 Add the meatballs. Bring to the boil, cover and simmer for 25–30 minutes or until the meatballs are cooked through. Serve on coriander rice and garnish with coriander sprigs.

Beef Vindaloo

A fiery hot dish originally from Goa, a "vindaloo" curry is made using a unique blend of hot aromatic spices and vinegar to give it a distinctive spicy flavour.

Serves 4

INGREDIENTS
15 ml/1 tbsp cumin seeds
4 dried red chillies
5 ml/1 tsp black peppercorns
5 green cardamom pods, seeds only
5 ml/1 tsp fenugreek seeds
5 ml/1 tsp black mustard seeds
2.5 ml/½ tsp salt
2.5 ml/½ tsp demerara sugar
60 ml/4 tbsp white wine vinegar
60 ml/4 tbsp oil
1 large onion, finely chopped
900 g/2 lb stewing beef, cut into
    2.5 cm/1 in cubes
2.5 cm/1 in piece root ginger,
    finely chopped
1 garlic clove, crushed
10 ml/2 tsp ground coriander
2.5 ml/½ tsp ground turmeric
plain and yellow rice, to serve

1 Put the cumin seeds, chillies, peppercorns, cardamom seeds, fenugreek seeds and mustard seeds into a coffee grinder or use a pestle and mortar and grind to a fine powder. Add the salt, sugar and white wine vinegar and mix to a thin paste.

2 Heat 30 ml/2 tbsp of the oil in a large frying pan and fry the onions for 10 minutes. Put the onions and the spice mixture into a food processor or blender and process to a coarse paste.

3 Heat the remaining oil in the frying pan and fry the meat cubes for about 10 minutes until lightly browned. Remove the beef cubes with a slotted spoon and set aside.

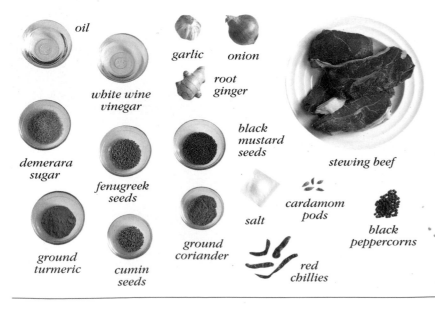

oil

garlic   onion

white wine vinegar

root ginger

black mustard seeds

demerara sugar

stewing beef

fenugreek seeds

salt

cardamom pods

ground turmeric

ground coriander

cumin seeds

black peppercorns

red chillies

4 Add the ginger and garlic and fry for 2 minutes. Stir in the ground coriander and turmeric and fry for 2 minutes.

5 Add the spice and onion paste and fry for about 5 minutes.

6 Return the meat to the pan together with 300 ml/¹/₂ pint/1¹/₄ cups water. Cover and simmer for 1–1¹/₂ hours or until the meat is tender. Serve with plain and yellow rice.

COOK'S TIP

To make plain and yellow rice, infuse a pinch of saffron strands or dissolve a little ground turmeric in 15 ml/1 tbsp hot water. Stir into half the cooked rice until uniformly yellow. Carefully mix the yellow rice into the plain rice.

Lamb Kebabs

First introduced by the Muslims, kebabs have now become a favourite Indian dish.

Serves 4

INGREDIENTS
FOR THE KEBABS
900 g/2 lb minced lamb
1 large onion, roughly chopped
5 cm/2 in piece root
    ginger, chopped
2 garlic cloves, crushed
1 green chilli, finely chopped
5 ml/1 tsp chilli powder
30 ml/2 tbsp chopped
    fresh coriander
5 ml/1 tsp garam masala
10 ml/2 tsp ground coriander
5 ml/1 tsp ground cumin
5 ml/1 tsp salt
1 egg, beaten
15 ml/1 tbsp natural yogurt
15 ml/1 tbsp oil
mixed salad leaves, to serve

FOR THE RAITA
250 ml/8 fl oz/1 cup
    natural yogurt
1/2 cucumber, finely chopped
30 ml/2 tbsp chopped fresh mint
1.5 ml/1/4 tsp salt

cucumber   garlic
natural
yogurt
garam
masala
ground
cumin   ground
         coriander   minced lamb
chilli
powder   fresh
         coriander   root ginger   mint
              egg
              onion   green
                            chilli

1 Put all the ingredients for the kebabs, except the yogurt and oil, into a food processor or blender and process until the mixture binds together. Spoon into a bowl and leave to marinate for 1 hour.

2 For the raita, mix together all the ingredients and chill for 15 minutes.

3 Preheat the grill. Divide the mixture into eight equal portions with lightly floured hands and mould into sausage shapes. Thread on to skewers and chill.

4 Brush the kebabs lightly with the yogurt and oil and cook under a hot grill for 8–10 minutes, turning occasionally, until brown all over. Serve the kebabs on a bed of mixed salad leaves accompanied by the raita.

Balti Beef

Balti curries are cooked and served in a two-handled pan known as a karahi and are traditionally served with naan bread. If you don't have a karahi then you can use a wok.

Serves 4

INGREDIENTS
1 red pepper
1 grcen pepper
30 ml/2 tbsp oil
5 ml/1 tsp cumin seeds
2.5 ml/½ tsp fennel secds
1 onion, cut into thick wedges
1 garlic clove, crushed
2.5 cm/1 in piece root ginger, finely chopped
1 red chilli, finely chopped
15 ml/1 tbsp curry paste
2.5 ml/½ tsp salt
675 g/1½ lb rump or fillet steak, cut into thick strips
coriander naan bread, to serve

oil   fennel seeds   green pepper

curry paste   red pepper

red chilli   onion   steak   salt

cumin seeds   garlic   root ginger

1 Cut the red and green peppers into 2.5 cm/1 in chunks.

2 Heat the oil in a wok or karahi and fry the cumin and fennel seeds for about 2 minutes or until they begin to splutter. Add the onion, garlic, ginger and chilli and fry for 5 minutes.

3 Add the curry paste and salt and fry for a further 3–4 minutes.

4 Add the peppers and stir-fry for about 5 minutes. Stir in the beef and continue to fry for 10–12 minutes or until the meat is tender. Serve with warm coriander naan bread.

Spicy Lamb and Potato Stew

Transform this simple dish into a tasty stew with the addition of Indian spices.

Serves 4

INGREDIENTS

675 g/1½ lb lamb fillet
45 ml/3 tbsp oil
1 onion, finely chopped
2 bay leaves
1 green chilli, seeded and
    finely chopped
2 garlic cloves, finely chopped
10 ml/2 tsp ground coriander
5 ml/1 tsp ground cumin
2.5 ml/½ tsp ground turmeric
2.5 ml/½ tsp chilli powder
2.5 ml/½ tsp salt
225 g/8 oz tomatoes, skinned and
    finely chopped
600 ml/1 pint/2½ cups lamb stock
2 large potatoes, cut into
    2.5 cm/1 in chunks
chopped fresh coriander, to garnish
chappatis, to serve

potatoes

lamb stock

oil

tomatoes

onion

ground
turmeric

ground
cumin

chilli
powder

lamb fillet

ground
coriander

salt

garlic

bay
leaves

green chilli

1 Remove any visible fat and cut the meat into 2.5 cm/1 in cubes.

2 Heat the oil in a large saucepan and fry the onion, bay leaves, chilli and garlic for 5 minutes.

3 Add the meat and cook for about 6–8 minutes until lightly browned.

4 Add the ground coriander, cumin, turmeric, chilli powder and salt and cook for 3–4 minutes, stirring all the time to prevent the spices from sticking.

5 Add the tomatoes and stock and simmer for 5 minutes until the sauce thickens. Bring to the boil, cover and simmer for 1 hour.

6 Add the potatoes and cook for a further 30–40 minutes or until the meat is tender. Garnish with chopped fresh coriander and serve with chappatis.

Chicken Tikka Masala

Tender chicken pieces cooked in a creamy, spicy tomato sauce and served on naan bread.

Serves 4

INGREDIENTS

675 g/1½ lb chicken breasts, skinned
90 ml/6 tbsp tikka paste
60 ml/4 tbsp natural yogurt
30 ml/2 tbsp oil
1 onion, chopped
1 garlic clove, crushed
1 green chilli, seeded and chopped
2.5 cm/1 in piece root ginger, grated
15 ml/1 tbsp tomato purée
15 ml/1 tbsp ground almonds
250 ml/8 fl oz/1 cup water
45 ml/3 tbsp butter, melted
50 ml/2 fl oz/¼ cup double cream
15 ml/1 tbsp lemon juice
fresh coriander sprigs, natural
    yogurt and toasted cumin seeds,
    to garnish
naan bread, to serve

onion
oil
double cream
butter
tikka paste
chicken breasts
root ginger
natural yogurt
lemon juice
green chilli
garlic
ground almonds
tomato purée

1 Cut the chicken into 2.5 cm/1 in cubes. Put 45 ml/3 tbsp of the tikka paste and all of the yogurt into a bowl. Add the chicken and leave to marinate for 20 minutes.

2 For the tikka sauce, heat the oil and fry the onion, garlic, chilli and ginger for 5 minutes. Add remaining tikka paste and fry for 2 minutes. Add the tomato purée, almonds and water, simmer 15 minutes.

3 Meanwhile, thread the chicken on to wooden kebab skewers. Preheat the grill.

4 Brush the chicken pieces with the butter and grill under a medium heat for 15 minutes, turning occasionally.

5 Put the tikka sauce into a food processor or blender and process until smooth. Return to the pan.

6 Add the cream and lemon juice, remove the chicken pieces from the skewers and add to the saucepan, then simmer for 5 minutes. Serve on naan bread and garnish with fresh coriander, yogurt and toasted cumin seeds.

COOK'S TIP
Soak the wooden skewers in cold water before using to prevent them from burning while grilling.

Tandoori Chicken

This classic Indian dish is traditionally cooked in the tandoor which is a vat-shaped clay oven, heated with charcoal or wood.

Serves 4

INGREDIENTS
8 chicken pieces, such as thighs, drumsticks, and halved breasts, skinned
60 ml/4 tbsp lemon juice
5 ml/1 tsp salt
2 garlic cloves, roughly chopped
2.5 cm/1 in piece root ginger, roughly chopped
2 green chillies, roughly chopped
175 ml/6 fl oz/¾ cup natural yogurt
5 ml/1 tsp salt
5 ml/1 tsp chilli powder
5 ml/1 tsp garam masala
5 ml/1 tsp ground cumin
5 ml/1 tsp ground coriander
red food colouring (optional)
30 ml/2 tbsp butter, melted
lemon wedges, to garnish
chilli powder and a sprig of fresh mint, to garnish
salad and Cucumber Raita, to serve

natural yogurt

ground cumin

ground coriander

butter

garam masala

lemon juice

chilli powder

chicken pieces

red food colouring

root ginger

green chilli

garlic

1 Cut deep slashes in the chicken pieces. Mix together the lemon juice and the salt and rub over the chicken. Leave to marinate for 10 minutes.

2 Put the garlic, ginger and chillies into a food processor or blender and process until smooth. Add the mixture to a bowl containing the yogurt, salt, chilli powder, garam masala, ground cumin and ground coriander, and mix well.

3 Brush the chicken pieces with food colouring, if using, and put into a dish. Add the marinade and chill overnight. Preheat the oven to 220°C/425°F/Gas 7. Put the chicken in a roasting tin and bake for 40 minutes, basting with butter. Serve with lemon, salad and Cucumber Raita, garnished with chilli powder and mint.

COOK'S TIP
The traditional bright red colour associated with this dish is derived from food colouring. This is only optional and may be omitted from the recipe if you wish.

Chicken Jalfrezi

A Jalfrezi curry is a stir-fried dish cooked with onions, ginger and garlic in a rich pepper sauce.

Serves 4

INGREDIENTS
675 g/1½ lb chicken breasts, skinned
30 ml/2 tbsp oil
5 ml/1 tsp cumin seeds
1 onion, finely chopped
1 green pepper, finely chopped
1 red pepper, finely chopped
1 garlic clove, crushed
2 cm/¾ in piece root ginger,
    finely chopped
15 ml/1 tbsp curry paste
1.5 ml/¼ tsp chilli powder
5 ml/1 tsp ground coriander
5 ml/1 tsp ground cumin
2.5 ml/½ tsp salt
400 g/14 oz can chopped tomatoes
30 ml/2 tbsp chopped
    fresh coriander
fresh coriander sprig, to garnish
plain rice, to serve

chopped tomatoes *red pepper* *green pepper*

oil *chilli powder* *garlic* *onion*

ground coriander

curry paste *chicken breasts*

ground cumin *cumin seeds* *root ginger* *salt* *fresh coriander*

1 Remove any visible fat and cut the chicken into 2.5 cm/1 in cubes.

2 Heat the oil in a wok and fry the cumin seeds for 2 minutes until they splutter. Add the onion, peppers, garlic and ginger and fry for 6–8 minutes.

3 Add the curry paste and fry for about 2 minutes. Stir in the chilli powder, ground coriander, cumin and salt and add 15 ml/1 tbsp water; fry for a further 2 minutes.

4 Add the chicken and fry for about 5 minutes. Add the tomatoes and fresh coriander. Cover and cook for about 15 minutes or until the chicken is tender. Serve with rice; garnish with coriander.

Coconut Chicken

A Goan-style curry made from a delicious blend of authentic Indian spices and toasted coconut.

Serves 4

INGREDIENTS

75 g/3 oz/1½ cups desiccated
    coconut
30 ml/2 tbsp oil
2.5 ml/½ tsp cumin seeds
4 black peppercorns
15 ml/1 tbsp fennel seeds
15 ml/1 tbsp coriander seeds
2 onions, finely chopped
2.5 ml/½ tsp salt
8 small chicken pieces, such as
    thighs and drumsticks, skinned
fresh coriander sprigs and
    lemon wedges, to garnish
Mint and Coconut Chutney, to serve

coriander seeds

desiccated coconut

oil

chicken pieces

fennel seeds

cumin seeds

black peppercorns

salt

onions

1 Put the desiccated coconut in a bowl with 45 ml/3 tbsp water. Leave to soak for 15 minutes.

2 Meanwhile, heat 15 ml/1 tbsp of the oil in a large frying pan and fry the cumin seeds, peppercorns, fennel and coriander seeds over a low heat for 3–4 minutes until the seeds begin to splutter.

3 Add the finely chopped onions and fry for about 5 minutes.

4 Stir in the coconut and salt and continue to fry for a further 5 minutes, stirring occasionally to prevent the mixture from sticking to the pan.

5 Put the coconut mixture into a food processor or blender and process to form a coarse paste. Spoon into a bowl and set aside until required.

6 Heat the remaining oil and fry the chicken for 10 minutes. Add the coconut paste and cook over a low heat for 15–20 minutes, or until the coconut mixture is golden brown and the chicken is tender. Garnish with sprigs of fresh coriander and lemon wedges and serve with Mint and Coconut Chutney.

COOK'S TIP
Make the spiced coconut mixture the day before and chill it in the fridge, then continue from the final step when required.

Chicken Dhansak

Dhansak curries originate from the Parsee community and are traditionally made with lentils and meat.

Serves 4

INGREDIENTS
75 g/3 oz/½ cup green lentils
475 ml/16 fl oz/2 cups stock
45 ml/3 tbsp oil
5 ml/1 tsp cumin seeds
2 curry leaves
1 onion, finely chopped
2.5 cm/1 in piece root
    ginger, chopped
1 green chilli, finely chopped
5 ml/1 tsp ground cumin
5 ml/1 tsp ground coriander
1.5 ml/¼ tsp salt
1.5 ml/¼ tsp chilli powder
400 g/14 oz can chopped tomatoes
8 chicken pieces, skinned
60 ml/4 tbsp chopped
    fresh coriander
5 ml/1 tsp garam masala
fresh coriander sprigs, to garnish
plain and yellow rice, to serve

vegetable stock
ground cumin
oil
onion
ground coriander
chilli powder
chicken pieces
garam masala
cumin seeds
green lentils
chopped tomatoes
fresh coriander
curry leaves
green chilli
root ginger

1 Rinse the lentils under cold running water. Put into a large heavy-based saucepan with the stock. Bring to the boil, cover and simmer for about 15–20 minutes. Drain and set aside.

2 Heat the oil in a large saucepan and fry the cumin seeds and curry leaves for 2 minutes. Add the onion, ginger and chilli and fry for about 5 minutes. Stir in the cumin, coriander, salt and chilli powder with 30 ml/2 tbsp water.

3 Add the tomatoes and the chicken. Cover and cook for 10–15 minutes.

4 Add the lentils and stock, fresh coriander and garam masala and cook for 10 minutes or until the chicken is tender. Garnish with coriander sprigs and serve with plain and yellow rice.

Hot Chilli Chicken

Not for the faint-hearted, this fiery, hot curry is made with a spicy chilli masala paste.

Serves 4

INGREDIENTS

30 ml/2 tbsp tomato purée
2 garlic cloves, roughly chopped
2 green chillies, roughly chopped
5 dried red chillies
2.5 ml/¹/₂ tsp salt
1.5 ml/¹/₄ tsp sugar
5 ml/1 tsp chilli powder
2.5 ml/¹/₂ tsp paprika
15 ml/1 tbsp curry paste
30 ml/2 tbsp oil
2.5 ml/¹/₂ tsp cumin seeds
1 onion, finely chopped
2 bay leaves
5 ml/1 tsp ground coriander
5 ml/1 tsp ground cumin
1.5 ml/¹/₄ tsp ground turmeric
400 g/14 oz can chopped tomatoes
150 ml/¹/₄ pint/²/₃ cup water
8 chicken thighs, skinned
5 ml/1 tsp garam masala
sliced green chillies, to garnish
chappatis and natural yogurt,
    to serve

chopped
tomatoes

ground
turmeric

ground
coriander

curry paste

paprika

garam
masala

tomato
purée

chicken thighs

chilli
powder

ground
cumin

garlic

cumin
seeds

onion

green
chillies

bay
leaves

red chillies

1 Put the tomato purée, garlic, green and dried red chillies, salt, sugar, chilli powder, paprika and curry paste into a food processor or blender and process to a smooth paste.

2 Heat the oil in a large saucepan and fry the cumin seeds for 2 minutes. Add the onion and bay leaves and fry for about 5 minutes.

3 Add the chilli paste and fry for 2–3 minutes. Add the remaining ground spices and cook for 2 minutes. Add the chopped tomatoes and water. Bring to the boil and simmer for 5 minutes until the sauce thickens.

4 Add the chicken and garam masala. Cover and simmer for 25–30 minutes until the chicken is tender. Serve with chappatis and natural yogurt, garnished with sliced green chillies.

Chicken Saag

A mildly spiced dish using a popular combination of spinach and chicken. This recipe is best made using fresh spinach but if this is unavailable then you can use frozen instead.

Serves 4

INGREDIENTS

225 g/8 oz fresh spinach leaves,
    washed but not dried
2.5 cm/1 in piece root ginger, grated
2 garlic cloves, crushed
1 green chilli, roughly chopped
200 ml/7 fl oz/ scant 1 cup water
30 ml/2 tbsp oil
2 bay leaves
1.5 ml/¼ tsp black peppercorns
1 onion, finely chopped
4 tomatoes, skinned and
    finely chopped
10 ml/2 tsp curry powder
5 ml/1 tsp salt
5 ml/1 tsp chilli powder
45 ml/3 tbsp natural yogurt
8 chicken thighs, skinned
natural yogurt and chilli powder,
    to garnish
masala naan, to serve

natural yogurt

curry powder

chilli powder

black peppercorns

chicken thighs

root ginger

spinach leaves

green chilli

onion

bay leaves

tomatoes

garlic

1 Cook the spinach, without water, in a tightly covered saucepan for 5 minutes. Put the spinach, ginger, garlic and chilli with 50 ml/2 fl oz/¼ cup of the water into a food processor or blender and process to a thick purée.

2 Heat the oil in a large saucepan, add the bay leaves and black peppercorns and fry for 2 minutes. Add the onion and fry for 6–8 minutes or until the onion has browned.

3 Add the tomatoes and simmer for about 5 minutes. Stir in the curry powder, salt and chilli powder and cook for 2 minutes.

4 Add the purée and 150 ml/¼ pint/⅔ cup water; simmer for 5 minutes.

5 Add the yogurt, 15 ml/1 tbsp at a time and simmer for 5 minutes.

6 Add the chicken. Cover and cook for 25–30 minutes or until the chicken is tender. Serve on masala naan, drizzle over some natural yogurt and dust with chilli powder.

Jeera Chicken

An aromatic dish with a delicious, distinctive taste of cumin. Serve simply with a salad and yogurt.

Serves 4

INGREDIENTS

45 ml/3 tbsp cumin seeds
45 ml/3 tbsp oil
2.5 ml/½ tsp black peppercorns
4 green cardamom pods
2 green chillies, finely chopped
2 garlic cloves, crushed
2.5 cm/1 in piece root ginger, grated
5 ml/1 tsp ground coriander
10 ml/2 tsp ground cumin
2.5 ml/½ tsp salt
8 chicken pieces, such as thighs and
    drumsticks, skinned
5 ml/1 tsp garam masala
fresh coriander and chilli powder,
    to garnish
Cucumber Raita, to serve

oil

black peppercorns

chicken pieces

garam masala

ground coriander

cumin seeds

root ginger

green chillies

ground cumin

salt

garlic

green cardamom pods

cinnamon stick

1 Dry-roast 15 ml/1 tbsp of the cumin seeds for 5 minutes and set aside.

2 Heat the oil in a large saucepan and fry the remaining cumin seeds, black peppercorns and cardamoms for about 2–3 minutes.

3 Add the chillies, garlic and ginger and fry for 2 minutes.

4 Add the coriander, cumin and salt and cook for 2–3 minutes.

5 Add the chicken. Cover and simmer for 20–25 minutes.

6 Add the garam masala and reserved toasted cumin seeds and cook for a further 5 minutes. Serve with Cucumber Raita, garnished with chilli powder and fresh coriander.

Balti Chicken Curry

Tender pieces of chicken are lightly cooked with fresh vegetables and aromatic spices in the traditional Balti style.

Serves 4

INGREDIENTS
675 g/1½ lb chicken breasts, skinned
30 ml/2 tbsp oil
2.5 ml/½ tsp cumin seeds
2.5 ml/½ tsp fennel seeds
1 onion, thickly sliced
2 garlic cloves, crushed
2.5 cm/1 in piece root ginger,
    finely chopped
15 ml/1 tbsp curry paste
225 g/8 oz broccoli, broken
    into florets
4 tomatoes, cut into thick wedges
5 ml/1 tsp garam masala
30 ml/2 tbsp chopped
    fresh coriander
naan bread, to serve

oil
garam masala
fennel seeds
curry paste
cumin seeds
chicken breasts
tomatoes
root ginger
onion
fresh coriander
broccoli
garlic

1 Remove any fat and cut the chicken into 2.5 cm/1 in cubes.

2 Heat the oil in a wok and fry the cumin and fennel seeds for 2 minutes until the seeds begin to splutter. Add the onion, garlic and ginger and cook for 5–7 minutes. Stir in the curry paste and cook for a further 2–3 minutes.

3 Add the broccoli florets and fry for about 5 minutes. Add the chicken cubes and fry for 5–8 minutes.

4 Add the tomatoes, garam masala and chopped coriander. Cook for a further 5–10 minutes or until the chicken is tender. Serve with naan bread.

Chicken Dopiazza

Dopiazza literally translates as "two onions" and describes this chicken dish in which two types of onions arc used at different stages during the cooking process.

Serves 4

INGREDIENTS
45 ml/3 tbsp oil
8 small onions, halved
2 bay leaves
8 green cardamom pods
4 cloves
3 dried red chillies
8 black peppercorns
2 onions, finely chopped
2 garlic cloves, crushed
2.5 cm/1 in piece root ginger,
    finely chopped
5 ml/1 tsp ground coriander
5 ml/1 tsp ground cumin
2.5 ml/½ tsp ground turmeric
5 ml/1 tsp chilli powder
2.5 ml/½ tsp salt
4 tomatoes, skinned and
    finely chopped
120 ml/4 fl oz/½ cup water
8 chicken pieces, such as thighs and
    drumsticks, skinned
plain rice, to serve

1 Heat 30 ml/2 tbsp of the oil in a large saucepan and fry the small onions for 10 minutes, or until golden brown. Remove and set aside.

chilli powder

ground coriander

ground cumin

black peppercorns

ground turmeric

chicken pieces

onions

tomatoes

cloves

bay leaves

garlic

cardamom pods

small onions

red chillies

root ginger

2 Add the remaining oil and fry the bay leaves, cardamoms, cloves, chillies and peppercorns for 2 minutes. Add the chopped onions, garlic and ginger and fry for 5 minutes. Stir in the ground spices and salt and cook for 2 minutes.

3 Add the tomatoes and the water and simmer for 5 minutes until the sauce thickens. Add the chicken and cook for about 15 minutes.

4 Add the reserved small onions, then cover and cook for a further 10 minutes, or until the chicken is tender. Serve with plain boiled rice.

COOK'S TIP

Soak the small onions in boiling water for 2–3 minutes to make them easier to peel.

Prawn Curry

A rich flavoursome curry made from prawns and a delicious blend of aromatic spices.

Serves 4

INGREDIENTS

675 g/1½ lb uncooked tiger prawns
4 dried red chillies
50 g/2 oz/1 cup desiccated coconut
5 ml/1 tsp black mustard seeds
1 large onion, chopped
45 ml/3 tbsp oil
4 bay leaves
2.5 cm/1 in piece root ginger,
   finely chopped
2 garlic cloves, crushed
15 ml/1 tbsp ground coriander
5 ml/1 tsp chilli powder
5 ml/1 tsp salt
4 tomatoes, finely chopped
plain rice, to serve

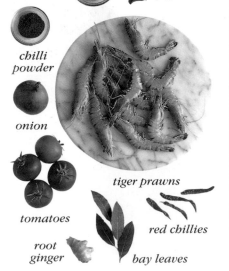

ground coriander *oil*
desiccated coconut
black mustard seeds *garlic*
chilli powder
onion
tiger prawns
tomatoes *red chillies*
root ginger *bay leaves*

2 Put the dried red chillies, coconut, mustard seeds and onion in a large frying pan and dry-fry for 8–10 minutes or until the mixture begins to brown. Put into a food processor or blender and process to a coarse paste.

1 Peel the prawns. Run a sharp knife along the back of each prawn to make a shallow cut and carefully remove the thin black intestinal vein.

3 Heat the oil in the frying pan and fry the bay leaves for 1 minute. Add the chopped ginger and the garlic and fry for 2–3 minutes.

4 Add the coriander, chilli powder, salt and the paste and fry for 5 minutes.

5 Stir in the tomatoes and about 175 ml/6 fl oz/¾ cup water and simmer for 5–6 minutes or until thickened.

6 Add the prawns and cook for about 4–5 minutes or until they turn pink and the edges are curling slightly. Serve with plain boiled rice.

COOK'S TIP
Serve some extra tiger prawns, unpeeled, on the edge of each plate for an attractive garnish. Cook them with the peeled prawns.

Green Fish Curry

This dish combines all the flavours of the East.

Serves 4

INGREDIENTS

1.5 ml/¼ tsp ground turmeric
30 ml/2 tbsp lime juice
pinch of salt
4 cod fillets, skinned and cut into
    5 cm/2 in chunks
1 onion, chopped
1 green chilli, roughly chopped
1 garlic clove, crushed
25 g/1 oz/¼ cup cashew nuts
2.5 ml/½ tsp fennel seeds
30 ml/2 tbsp desiccated coconut
30 ml/2 tbsp oil
1.5 ml/¼ tsp cumin seeds
1.5 ml/¼ tsp ground coriander
1.5 ml/¼ tsp ground cumin
1.5 ml/¼ tsp salt
150 ml/¼ pint/⅔ cup water
175 ml/6 fl oz/¾ cup single cream
45 ml/3 tbsp finely chopped
    fresh coriander
Vegetable Pilau, to serve
fresh coriander sprig, to garnish

single cream
ground coriander
fennel seeds
ground turmeric
lime juice
desiccated coconut
cashew nuts
ground cumin
onion
cumin seeds
cod fillets
fresh coriander
green chilli
garlic

1 Mix together the turmeric, lime juice and salt and rub over the fish. Cover and leave to marinate for 15 minutes.

2 Meanwhile process the onion, chilli, garlic, cashew nuts, fennel seeds and coconut to a paste. Spoon the paste into a bowl and set aside.

3 Heat the oil in a large frying pan and fry the cumin seeds for 2 minutes until they begin to splutter. Add the paste and fry for 5 minutes then stir in the ground coriander, cumin, salt and water and fry for about 2–3 minutes.

4 Add the single cream and the fresh coriander. Simmer for 5 minutes. Add the fish and gently stir in. Cover and cook gently for 10 minutes until the fish is tender. Serve with Vegetable Pilau, garnished with a coriander sprig.

Indian Fish Stew

A spicy fish stew made with potatoes, peppers and traditional Indian spices.

Serves 4

INGREDIENTS
30 ml/2 tbsp oil
5 ml/1 tsp cumin seeds
1 onion, chopped
1 red pepper, thinly sliced
1 garlic clove, crushed
2 red chillies, finely chopped
2 bay leaves
2.5 ml/¹/₂ tsp salt
5 ml/1 tsp ground cumin
5 ml/1 tsp ground coriander
5 ml/1 tsp chilli powder
400 g/14 oz can chopped tomatoes
2 large potatoes, cut into
  2.5 cm/1 in chunks
300 ml/¹/₂ pint/1¹/₄ cups fish stock
4 cod fillets
chappatis, to serve

chopped tomatoes
ground cumin
chilli powder
fish stock
ground coriander
oil
cumin seeds
red pepper
onion
cod fillets
garlic
red chillies
potatoes
bay leaves
salt

1 Heat the oil in a large deep-sided frying pan and fry the cumin seeds for 2 minutes until they begin to splutter. Add the onion, pepper, garlic, chillies and bay leaves and fry for 5–7 minutes until the onions have browned.

2 Add the salt, ground cumin, ground coriander and chilli powder and cook for 3–4 minutes.

3 Stir in the tomatoes, potatoes and fish stock. Bring to the boil and simmer for a further 10 minutes.

4 Add the fish, then cover and simmer for 10 minutes, or until the fish is tender. Serve with chappatis.

Tuna Fish Curry

This unusual fish curry can be made in minutes.

Serves 4

INGREDIENTS
1 onion
1 red pepper
1 green pepper
45 ml/3 tbsp oil
1.5 ml/¼ tsp cumin seeds
2.5 ml/½ tsp ground cumin
2.5 ml/½ tsp ground coriander
2.5 ml/½ tsp chilli powder
1.5 ml/¼ tsp salt
2 garlic cloves, crushed
400 g/14 oz can tuna, drained
1 green chilli, finely chopped
2.5 cm/1 in piece root ginger, grated
1.5 ml/¼ tsp garam masala
5 ml/1 tsp lemon juice
30 ml/2 tbsp chopped
    fresh coriander
fresh coriander sprig, to garnish
pitta bread and Cucumber Raita,
    to serve

tuna

garam
masala

red pepper

cumin
seeds

green pepper

oil

ground
coriander

onion

lemon
juice

root ginger

ground
cumin

chilli
powder

green chilli

salt

garlic

1 Thinly slice the onion and the red and green peppers.

2 Heat the oil in a large frying pan and fry the cumin seeds for 2 minutes until they begin to splutter.

3 Add the cumin, coriander, chilli powder and salt; cook for 2–3 minutes. Add the garlic, onion and peppers.

4 Fry the vegetables, stirring from time to time, for 5–7 minutes until the onions have browned.

5 Stir in the tuna, chilli and ginger and cook for 5 minutes.

COOK'S TIP
Place the pitta bread on a grill rack and grill until it just puffs up. It will then be easy to split with a sharp knife.

6 Add the garam masala, lemon juice and fresh coriander and continue to cook for a further 3–4 minutes. Serve in warmed, split pitta bread with the Cucumber Raita garnished with a coriander sprig.

Goan-style Mussels

This is a simple way to cook mussels in a delicious fragrant coconut sauce.

Serves 4

INGREDIENTS
900 g/2 lb live mussels
115 g/4 oz creamed coconut
45 ml/3 tbsp oil
1 onion, finely chopped
3 garlic cloves, crushed
2.5 cm/1 in piece root ginger,
    finely chopped
2.5 ml/¹/₂ tsp ground turmeric
5 ml/1 tsp ground cumin
5 ml/1 tsp ground coriander
1.5 ml/¹/₄ tsp salt
chopped fresh coriander, to garnish

oil

ground turmeric

creamed coconut

ground coriander

live mussels

ground cumin

onion

root ginger

garlic

salt

1 Scrub the mussels under cold water and remove the beards. Discard any mussels that are already open.

2 Dissolve the creamed coconut in 450 ml/³/₄ pint/1 ³/₄ cups boiling water and set aside until needed.

3 Heat the oil in a large pan and fry the onion for 5 minutes. Add the garlic and ginger and fry for 2 minutes. Stir in the turmeric, cumin, coriander and salt and fry for a further 2 minutes. Add the creamed coconut liquid, bring to the boil and simmer for 5 minutes.

4 Add the mussels, cover and cook for 6–8 minutes or until all the mussels are cooked and open. Spoon the mussels on to a serving platter and pour the sauce over, then garnish with the chopped fresh coriander.

Coconut Salmon

This is an ideal dish to serve at dinner parties.

Serves 4

INGREDIENTS

10 ml/2 tsp ground cumin
10 ml/2 tsp chilli powder
2.5 ml/^{1}/$_2$ tsp ground turmeric
30 ml/2 tbsp white wine vinegar
1.5 ml/^{1}/$_4$ tsp salt
4 salmon steaks, about
   175 g/6 oz each
45 ml/3 tbsp oil
1 onion, chopped
2 green chillies, seeded
   and chopped
2 garlic cloves, crushed
2.5 cm/1 in piece root ginger, grated
5 ml/1 tsp ground coriander
175 ml/6 fl oz/^{3}/$_4$ cup coconut milk
spring onion rice, to serve
fresh coriander sprigs, to garnish

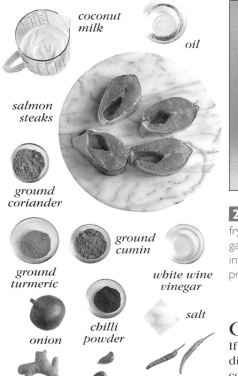

coconut
milk

oil

salmon
steaks

ground
coriander

ground
cumin

ground
turmeric

white wine
vinegar

salt

onion

chilli
powder

root ginger

garlic

green chillies

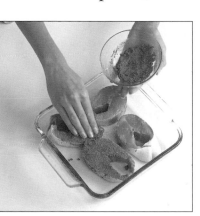

1 Mix 5 ml/1 tsp of the ground cumin together with the chilli powder, turmeric, vinegar and salt. Rub the paste over the salmon steaks and leave to marinate for about 15 minutes.

2 Heat the oil in a large deep-sided frying pan and fry the onion, chillies, garlic and ginger for 5–6 minutes. Put into a food processor or blender and process to a paste.

COOK'S TIP

If coconut milk is unavailable, dissolve some grated creamed coconut in boiling water and strain into a jug.

3 Return the paste to the pan. Add the remaining cumin, coriander and coconut milk. Bring to the boil and simmer for 5 minutes.

4 Add the salmon steaks. Cover and cook for 15 minutes until the fish is tender. Serve with spring onion rice and garnish with coriander.

Fish and Okra Curry

An interesting combination of flavours and textures is used to make this delicious fish dish.

Serves 4

INGREDIENTS

450 g/1 lb monkfish
5 ml/1 tsp ground turmeric
2.5 ml/¹/₂ tsp chilli powder
2.5 ml/¹/₂ tsp salt
5 ml/1 tsp cumin seeds
2.5 ml/¹/₂ tsp fennel seeds
2 dried red chillies
45 ml/3 tbsp oil
1 onion, finely chopped
2 garlic cloves, crushed
4 tomatoes, skinned and
    finely chopped
150 ml/¹/₄ pint/²/₃ cup water
225 g/8 oz okra, trimmed and cut
    into 2.5 cm/1 in lengths
5 ml/1 tsp garam masala
tomato rice, to serve

fennel seeds

cumin seeds *oil* *ground turmeric*

garam masala

chilli powder

okra

monkfish

tomatoes

onion *red chillies*

1 Remove the membrane and bones from the monkfish, cut into 2.5 cm/1 in cubes and place in a dish. Mix together the turmeric, chilli powder and 1.5 ml/¹/₄ tsp of the salt and rub the mixture all over the fish. Marinate for 15 minutes.

2 Put the cumin seeds, fennel seeds and chillies in a large frying pan and dry-roast for 3–4 minutes. Put into a blender or use a pestle and mortar and grind to a coarse powder.

3 Heat 30 ml/2 tbsp of the oil in the frying pan and and fry the fish for about 4–5 minutes. Remove with a slotted spoon and drain on kitchen paper.

4 Add the remaining oil to the pan and fry the onion and garlic for about 5 minutes. Add the spice powder and remaining salt and fry for 2–3 minutes. Stir in the tomatoes and water and simmer for 5 minutes.

5 Add the prepared okra and cook for about 5–7 minutes.

6 Return the fish to the pan together with the garam masala. Cover and simmer for 5–6 minutes or until the fish is tender. Serve with tomato rice.

COOK'S TIP
Yellow and plain rice would also go well with this curry, making an attractive presentation. Or serve it with plain rice, if you prefer.

Aloo Gobi

Cauliflower and potatoes are encrusted with Indian spices in this delicious recipe.

Serves 4

INGREDIENTS
450 g/1 lb potatoes, cut into
    2.5 cm/1 in chunks
30 ml/2 tbsp oil
5 ml/1 tsp cumin seeds
1 green chilli, finely chopped
450 g/1 lb cauliflower, broken
    into florets
5 ml/1 tsp ground coriander
5 ml/1 tsp ground cumin
1.5 ml/¼ tsp chilli powder
2.5 ml/½ tsp ground turmeric
2.5 ml/½ tsp salt
chopped fresh coriander, to garnish
tomato and onion salad and pickle,
    to serve

oil   *ground coriander*   *chilli powder*

ground cumin   *cumin seeds*   *ground turmeric*

salt

cauliflower

green chilli   *potatoes*

1 Par-boil the potatoes in a large saucepan of boiling water for 10 minutes. Drain well and set aside.

2 Heat the oil in a large frying pan and fry the cumin seeds for 2 minutes until they begin to splutter. Add the chilli and fry for a further 1 minute.

3 Add the cauliflower florets and fry, stirring, for 5 minutes.

4 Add the potatoes and the ground spices and salt and cook for a further 7–10 minutes, or until both the vegetables are tender. Garnish with fresh coriander and serve with tomato and onion salad and pickle.

VARIATION

Try using sweet potatoes instead of ordinary potatoes for an alternative curry with a sweeter flavour.

Masala Okra

Okra, or "ladies' fingers" are a popular Indian vegetable. In this recipe they are stir-fried with a dry, spicy masala to make a delicious side dish.

Serves 4

INGREDIENTS
450 g/1 lb okra
2.5 ml/½ tsp ground turmeric
5 ml/1 tsp chilli powder
15 ml/1 tbsp ground cumin
15 ml/1 tbsp ground coriander
1.5 ml/¼ tsp salt
1.5 ml/¼ tsp sugar
15 ml/1 tbsp lemon juice
15 ml/1 tbsp desiccated coconut
30 ml/2 tbsp chopped
   fresh coriander
45 ml/3 tbsp oil
2.5 ml/½ tsp cumin seeds
2.5 ml/½ tsp black mustard seeds
chopped fresh tomatoes, to garnish
poppadums, to serve

black mustard seeds   *lemon juice*   *ground coriander*   *cumin seeds*

ground cumin

chilli powder

sugar

ground turmeric   *okra*

desiccated coconut

salt   *fresh coriander*

COOK'S TIP
When buying okra, choose firm, brightly coloured pods that are less than 10 cm/4 in long.

1 Wash, dry and trim the okra. In a bowl, mix together the turmeric, chilli powder, cumin, ground coriander, salt, sugar, lemon juice, desiccated coconut and the fresh coriander.

2 Heat the oil in a large frying pan. Add the cumin seeds and mustard seeds and fry for about 2 minutes, or until they begin to splutter.

3 Add the spice mixture and continue to fry for 2 minutes.

4 Add the okra, cover, and cook over a low heat for 10 minutes, or until tender. Garnish with chopped fresh tomatoes and serve with poppadums.

Mixed Vegetable Curry

A good all-round vegetable curry that goes well with most Indian meat dishes. You can use any combination of vegetables that are in season for this basic recipe.

Serves 4

INGREDIENTS

30 ml/2 tbsp oil
2.5 ml/½ tsp black mustard seeds
2.5 ml/½ tsp cumin seeds
1 onion, thinly sliced
2 curry leaves
1 green chilli, finely chopped
2.5 cm/1 in piece root ginger, finely chopped
30 ml/2 tbsp curry paste
1 small cauliflower, broken into florets
1 large carrot, thickly sliced
115 g/4 oz French beans, cut into 2.5 cm/1 in lengths
1.5 ml/¼ tsp ground turmeric
1.5 ml/¼ tsp chilli powder
2.5 ml/½ tsp salt
2 tomatoes, finely chopped
50 g/2 oz frozen peas, thawed
150 ml/¼ pint/⅔ cup vegetable stock
fresh curry leaves, to garnish

vegetable stock *curry paste* *peas* *black mustard seeds* *chilli powder* *cauliflower* *ground turmeric* *cumin seeds* *tomatoes* *root ginger* *French beans* *carrot* *curry leaves* *onion* *green chilli*

1 Heat the oil in a large saucepan and fry the mustard seeds and cumin seeds for 2 minutes until they begin to splutter.

2 Add the onion and the curry leaves and fry for 5 minutes.

3 Add the chilli and ginger and fry for 2 minutes. Stir in the curry paste and fry for 3–4 minutes.

4 Add the cauliflower, carrot and French beans and cook for 4–5 minutes. Add the turmeric, chilli powder, salt and tomatoes and cook for 2–3 minutes..

5 Add the thawed peas and cook for a further 2–3 minutes.

6 Add the stock. Cover and simmer over a low heat for 10–13 minutes until all the vegetables are tender. Serve, garnished with curry leaves.

Banana Curry

An unusual partnership, but the sweetness of bananas combines well with the spices used, producing a mild, sweet curry. Choose bananas that are slightly under-ripe so that they retain their shape and do not become mushy.

Serves 4

INGREDIENTS
4 under-ripe bananas
30 ml/2 tbsp ground coriander
15 ml/1 tbsp ground cumin
5 ml/1 tsp chilli powder
2.5 ml/½ tsp salt
1.5 ml/¼ tsp ground turmeric
5 ml/1 tsp sugar
15 ml/1 tbsp gram flour
45 ml/3 tbsp chopped
    fresh coriander
90 ml/6 tbsp oil
1.5 ml/¼ tsp cumin seeds
1.5 ml/¼ tsp black mustard seeds
fresh coriander sprigs, to garnish
chappatis, to serve

oil

ground turmeric *chilli powder*

gram flour *cumin seeds*

ground coriander

bananas *black mustard seeds*

sugar *ground cumin*

salt *fresh coriander*

1 Trim the bananas and cut each into three equal pieces leaving the skin on. Make a lengthways slit in each piece of banana, without cutting through.

2 Mix together on a plate, the coriander, cumin, chilli powder, salt, turmeric, sugar, gram flour, fresh coriander and 15 ml/1 tbsp of the oil.

3 Carefully stuff each piece of banana with the spice mixture, taking care not to break them in half.

4 Heat the remaining oil in a large heavy-based saucepan and fry the cumin and mustard seeds for 2 minutes or until they begin to splutter. Add the bananas and toss gently in the oil. Cover and simmer over a low heat for 15 minutes stirring from time to time until the bananas are soft, but not mushy. Garnish with the fresh coriander and serve with warm chappatis.

Aubergine Curry

A simple and delicious way of cooking aubergines which retains their full flavour.

Serves 4

INGREDIENTS
2 large aubergines, about
    450 g/1 lb each
45 ml/3 tbsp oil
2.5 ml/½ tsp black mustard seeds
1 bunch spring onions,
    finely chopped
115 g/4 oz button
    mushrooms, halved
2 garlic cloves, crushed
1 red chilli, finely chopped
2.5 ml/½ tsp chilli powder
5 ml/1 tsp ground cumin
5 ml/1 tsp ground coriander
1.5 ml/¼ tsp ground turmeric
5 ml/ 1 tsp salt
400 g/14 oz can chopped tomatoes
15 ml/1 tbsp chopped
    fresh coriander
fresh coriander sprig, to garnish

black mustard seeds — ground turmeric — chopped tomatoes — chilli powder — ground cumin — fresh coriander — button mushrooms — ground coriander — aubergines — garlic — spring onions — red chilli

1 Preheat the oven to 200°C/400°F/ Gas 6. Brush both of the aubergines with 15 ml/1 tbsp of the oil and prick with a fork. Bake in the oven for 30–35 minutes until the aubergines are soft.

2 Meanwhile, heat the remaining oil in a saucepan and fry the mustard seeds for 2 minutes until they begin to splutter. Add the onions, mushrooms, garlic and chilli and fry for 5 minutes. Stir in the chilli powder, cumin, coriander, turmeric and salt and fry for 3–4 minutes. Add the tomatoes and simmer for 5 minutes.

3 Cut each of the aubergines in half lengthways and scoop out the soft flesh into a bowl. Mash the flesh briefly.

COOK'S TIP
If you want to omit the oil, wrap the aubergines in foil and bake in the oven for 1 hour.

4 Add the mashed aubergines and fresh coriander to the saucepan. Bring to the boil and simmer for 5 minutes or until the sauce thickens. Serve, garnished with a fresh coriander sprig.

Sweetcorn and Pea Curry

Tender sweetcorn is cooked in a spicy tomato
sauce. Use fresh sweetcorn when it is in season.

Serves 4

INGREDIENTS
6 pieces of frozen corn on the cob
45 ml/3 tbsp oil
2.5 ml/½ tsp cumin seeds
1 onion, finely chopped
2 garlic cloves, crushed
1 green chilli, finely chopped
15 ml/1 tbsp curry paste
5 ml/1 tsp ground coriander
5 ml/1 tsp ground cumin
1.5 ml/¼ tsp ground turmeric
2.5 ml/½ tsp salt
2.5 ml/½ tsp sugar
400 g/14 oz can chopped tomatoes
15 ml/1 tbsp tomato purée
150 ml/¼ pint/⅔ cup water
115 g/4 oz frozen peas, thawed
30 ml/2 tbsp chopped
    fresh coriander
chappatis, to serve (optional)

peas

chopped
tomatoes

pieces of corn
on the cob

oil

sugar

tomato
purée

ground
turmeric

ground
coriander

cumin
seeds

curry paste

ground
cumin

salt

garlic

onion

green chilli

fresh coriander

1 Use a sharp knife and cut each piece
of corn in half crossways to make
12 equal pieces in total.

2 Bring a large saucepan of water to
the boil and cook the corn cob pieces
for 10–12 minutes. Drain well.

3 Heat the oil in large saucepan and
fry the cumin seeds for 2 minutes or
until they begin to splutter. Add the
onion, garlic and chilli and fry for about
5–6 minutes until the onions are golden.

4 Add the curry paste and fry for
2 minutes. Stir in the remaining spices,
salt and sugar and fry for 2–3 minutes.

5 Add the chopped tomatoes and
tomato purée together with the water
and simmer for 5 minutes or until the
sauce thickens. Add the peas and cook
for a further 5 minutes.

6 Add the pieces of corn and fresh
coriander and cook for a further 6–8
minutes or until the corn and peas are
tender. Serve with chappatis, for
mopping up the rich sauce, if you like.

VARIATION
If you don't like peas then you can
replace them with the same quantity
of frozen sweetcorn.

Aloo Saag

Spinach, potatoes and traditional Indian spices are the main ingredients in this simple, delicious and authentic curry.

Serves 4

INGREDIENTS
450 g/1 lb spinach
30 ml/2 tbsp oil
5 ml/1 tsp black mustard seeds
1 onion, thinly sliced
2 garlic cloves, crushed
2.5 cm/1 in piece root ginger, finely chopped
675 g/1½ lb potatoes, cut into 2.5 cm/1 in chunks
5 ml/1 tsp chilli powder
5 ml/1 tsp salt
120 ml/4 fl oz/½ cup water

onion *oil*

black mustard seeds

chilli powder

root ginger

spinach

salt

garlic

potatoes

1 Wash the spinach then blanch in boiling water for 3–4 minutes.

COOK'S TIP

To make certain that the spinach is dry, put it in a clean dish towel, roll up tightly and squeeze gently to remove any excess liquid.

2 Drain the spinach thoroughly and set aside. When it is cool enough to handle, use your hands to squeeze out any remaining liquid.

3 Heat the oil in a large saucepan and fry the mustard seeds for 2 minutes or until they begin to splutter.

4 Add the onion, garlic and ginger and fry for 5 minutes, stirring.

5 Add the potatoes, chilli powder, salt and water and cook for 8 minutes.

6 Add the spinach. Cover and simmer for 10–15 minutes or until the potatoes are tender. Serve hot.

COOK'S TIP
Use a waxy variety of potato for this dish so the pieces do not break up during cooking.

Mushroom Curry

This is a delicious way of cooking mushrooms which goes well with any meat dish.

Serves 4

INGREDIENTS
30 ml/2 tbsp oil
2.5 ml/½ tsp cumin seeds
1.5 ml/¼ tsp black peppercorns
4 green cardamom pods
1.5 ml/¼ tsp ground turmeric
1 onion, finely chopped
5 ml/1 tsp ground cumin
5 ml/1 tsp ground coriander
2.5 ml/½ tsp garam masala
1 green chilli, finely chopped
2 garlic cloves, crushed
2.5 cm/1 in piece root ginger, grated
400 g/14 oz can chopped tomatoes
1.5 ml/¼ tsp salt
450 g/1 lb button mushrooms, halved
chopped fresh coriander, to garnish

chopped tomatoes
oil
ground turmeric
cumin seeds
black peppercorns
ground coriander
garam masala
ground cumin
onion
button mushrooms
salt
root ginger
green chilli
cardamom pods
garlic

1 Heat the oil in a large saucepan and fry the cumin seeds, peppercorns, cardamom pods and turmeric for 2–3 minutes.

2 Add the onion and fry for about 5 minutes until golden. Stir in the cumin, coriander and garam masala and fry for a further 2 minutes.

3 Add the chilli, garlic and ginger and fry for 2–3 minutes stirring all the time to prevent the spices from sticking to the pan. Add the tomatoes and salt. Bring to the boil and simmer for 5 minutes.

4 Add the mushrooms. Cover and simmer over a low heat for 10 minutes. Garnish with chopped fresh coriander. This curry would be good with Spicy Lamb and Potato Stew.

Spicy Bitter Gourds

Bitter gourds are widely used in Indian cooking, both on their own and combined with other vegetables in a curry.

Serves 4

INGREDIENTS

675 g/1½ lb bitter gourds
60 ml/4 tbsp oil
2.5 ml/½ tsp cumin seeds
6 spring onions, finely chopped
5 tomatoes, finely chopped
2.5 cm/1 in piece root ginger, finely chopped
2 garlic cloves, crushed
2 green chillies, finely chopped
2.5 ml/½ tsp salt
2.5 ml/½ tsp chilli powder
5 ml/1 tsp ground coriander
5 ml/1 tsp ground cumin
45 ml/3 tbsp peanuts, crushed
45 ml/3 tbsp soft dark brown sugar
15 ml/1 tbsp gram flour
fresh coriander sprigs, to garnish

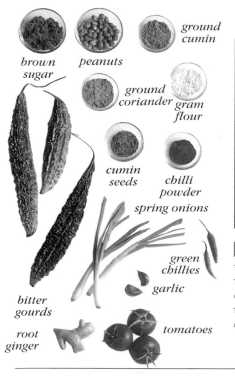

brown sugar
peanuts
ground cumin
ground coriander
gram flour
cumin seeds
chilli powder
spring onions
green chillies
garlic
bitter gourds
root ginger
tomatoes

1 Bring a large pan of lightly salted water to the boil. Peel the bitter gourds using a small sharp knife and halve them. Discard the seeds. Cut into 2 cm/¾ in pieces then cook in the water for about 10–15 minutes, or until they are tender. Drain well and set aside.

2 Heat the oil in a large saucepan and fry the cumin seeds for 2 minutes until they begin to splutter. Add the spring onions and fry for 3–4 minutes. Add the tomatoes, ginger, garlic and chillies and cook for 5 minutes.

3 Add the salt, remaining spices, the peanuts and sugar and cook for about 2–3 minutes.

COOK'S TIP

For a quick and easy way to crush peanuts, put into a food processor or blender and process for about 20–30 seconds.

4 Add the bitter gourds and mix well. Sprinkle over the gram flour. Cover and simmer over a low heat for 5–8 minutes or until all of the gram flour has been absorbed into the sauce. Serve garnished with fresh coriander sprigs.

Spicy Potato Chips with Sesame Seeds

This recipe is a variation of the well-known dish Bombay Potatoes, in which the potatoes are fried to give them a crispy texture, and then tossed in spices and sesame seeds.

Serves 4

INGREDIENTS
900 g/2 lb potatoes
oil, for deep-frying
1.5 ml/¼ tsp ground turmeric
1.5 ml/¼ tsp chilli powder
1.5 ml/¼ tsp salt
30 ml/2 tbsp oil
1.5 ml/¼ tsp black mustard seeds
1 green chilli, finely chopped
1 garlic clove, crushed
30 ml/2 tbsp sesame seeds

oil

black mustard
seeds

sesame
seeds

ground
turmeric

chilli
powder

green
chilli

potatoes

garlic

salt

1 Cut the potatoes into thick chips.

2 Heat the oil for deep-frying to 160°C/325°F. Fry the chips in batches for 5 minutes, until golden. Drain well on plenty of kitchen paper.

3 Put the chips in a bowl and sprinkle over the turmeric, chilli powder and salt. Cool, then toss the chips in the spices until they are evenly coated.

4 Heat the 30 ml/2 tbsp oil in a large saucepan and fry the mustard seeds for 2 minutes until they splutter. Add the chilli and garlic and fry for 2 minutes.

5 Add the sesame seeds and fry for 3–4 minutes until the seeds begin to brown. Remove from the heat.

6 Add the sesame seed mixture to the potatoes and toss together to coat evenly. Serve cold, or reheat for about 5 minutes in an oven preheated to 200°C/400°F/Gas 6.

COOK'S TIP
Make sure the chips are as uniform in size as possible to ensure that they cook evenly.

Courgette Curry

Thickly sliced courgettes are combined with authentic Indian spices for a delicious, colourful vegetable curry.

Serves 4

INGREDIENTS
675 g/1½ lb courgettes
45 ml/3 tbsp oil
2.5 ml/½ tsp cumin seeds
2.5 ml/½ tsp mustard seeds
1 onion, thinly sliced
2 garlic cloves, crushed
1.5 ml/¼ tsp ground turmeric
1.5 ml/¼ tsp chilli powder
5 ml/1 tsp ground coriander
5 ml/1 tsp ground cumin
2.5 ml/½ tsp salt
15 ml/1 tbsp tomato purée
400 g/14 oz can chopped tomatoes
150 ml/¼ pint/⅔ cup water
15 ml/1 tbsp chopped
 fresh coriander
5 ml/1 tsp garam masala

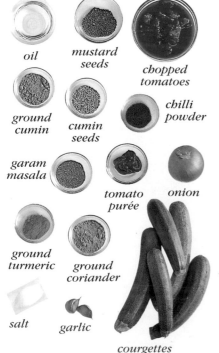

oil   mustard seeds   chopped tomatoes

ground cumin   cumin seeds   chilli powder

garam masala   tomato purée   onion

ground turmeric   ground coriander

salt   garlic

courgettes

1 Trim the ends from the courgettes then cut into 1 cm/½ in thick slices.

2 Heat the oil in a large saucepan and fry the cumin and mustard seeds for 2 minutes until they begin to splutter.

3 Add the onion and garlic and fry for about 5–6 minutes.

4 Add the turmeric, chilli powder, coriander, cumin and salt and fry for about 2–3 minutes.

fresh coriander

5 Add the sliced courgettes all at once, and cook for 5 minutes.

6 Mix together the tomato purée and chopped tomatoes and add to the saucepan with the water. Cover and simmer for 10 minutes until the sauce thickens. Stir in the fresh coriander and garam masala, then cook for 5 minutes or until the courgettes are tender.

Vegetable Kashmiri

This is a delicious vegetable curry, in which fresh mixed vegetables are cooked in a spicy, aromatic yogurt sauce.

Serves 4

INGREDIENTS

10 ml/2 tsp cumin seeds
8 black peppercorns
2 green cardamom pods, seeds only
5 cm/2 in cinnamon stick
2.5 ml/¹/₂ tsp grated nutmeg
45 ml/3 tbsp oil
1 green chilli, chopped
2.5 cm/1 in piece root ginger, grated
5 ml/1 tsp chilli powder
2.5 ml/¹/₂ tsp salt
2 large potatoes, cut into
    2.5 cm/1 in chunks
225 g/8 oz cauliflower, broken
    into florets
225 g/8 oz okra, thickly sliced
150 ml/¹/₄ pint/²/₃ cup natural yogurt
150 ml/¹/₄ pint/²/₃ cup
    vegetable stock
toasted flaked almonds and fresh
    coriander sprigs, to garnish

vegetable stock

oil

chilli powder

black peppercorns

cauliflower

potatoes

cumin seeds

cinnamon stick

natural yogurt

salt

nutmeg

root ginger

okra

cardamom pods

green chilli

1 Grind the cumin seeds, peppercorns, cardamom seeds, cinnamon stick and nutmeg to a fine powder using a blender or a pestle and mortar.

2 Heat the oil in a large saucepan and fry the chilli and ginger for 2 minutes, stirring all the time.

3 Add the chilli powder, salt and ground spice mixture and fry for about 2–3 minutes, stirring all the time to prevent the spices from sticking.

4 Stir in the potatoes, cover, and cook for 10 minutes over a low heat, stirring from time to time.

5 Add the cauliflower and okra and cook for 5 minutes.

6 Add the yogurt and stock. Bring to the boil, then reduce the heat. Cover and simmer for 20 minutes, or until all the vegetables are tender. Garnish with toasted almonds and coriander sprigs.

Stuffed Baby Vegetables

The combination of potatoes and aubergines is popular in Indian cooking. This recipe uses small, baby vegetables which are stuffed with a dry, spicy masala paste.

Serves 4

INGREDIENTS
12 small potatoes
8 baby aubergines

FOR THE STUFFING
15 ml/1 tbsp sesame seeds
30 ml/2 tbsp ground coriander
30 ml/2 tbsp ground cumin
2.5 ml/½ tsp salt
1.5 ml/¼ tsp chilli powder
2.5 ml/½ tsp ground turmeric
10 ml/2 tsp sugar
1.5 ml/¼ tsp garam masala
15 ml/1 tbsp peanuts,
    roughly crushed
15 ml/1 tbsp gram flour
2 garlic cloves, crushed
15 ml/1 tbsp lemon juice
30 ml/2 tbsp chopped
    fresh coriander

FOR THE SAUCE
30 ml/2 tbsp oil
2.5 ml/½ tsp black mustard seeds
400 g/14 oz can chopped tomatoes
30 ml/2 tbsp chopped
    fresh coriander
150 ml/¼ pint/⅔ cup water
single cream, to garnish (optional)

1 Preheat the oven to 200°C/400°F/ Gas 6. Make slits in the potatoes and aubergines making sure that you do not cut right through.

2 Mix all the ingredients for the stuffing together on a plate.

3 Carefully stuff the potatoes and aubergines with the spice mixture.

chopped tomatoes

baby aubergines

oil

peanuts

garam masala

ground turmeric

sesame seeds

black mustard seeds

chilli powder

fresh coriander

salt

small potatoes

gram flour

lemon juice

sugar

ground coriander

garlic

ground cumin

4 Place the potatoes and aubergines in a greased ovenproof dish.

5 Heat the oil in a saucepan and fry the mustard seeds for 2 minutes until they begin to splutter, then add the tomatoes, coriander and any leftover stuffing together with the water. Simmer for 5 minutes until the sauce thickens.

6 Pour the sauce over the potatoes and aubergines. Cover and bake for 25–30 minutes until the potatoes and aubergines are soft. Garnish with single cream, if using.

Masala Chana

Chick-peas are used and cooked in a variety of ways all over the Indian sub-continent. Tamarind gives this dish a deliciously sharp, tangy flavour.

COOK'S TIP
To save time, make double the quantity of tamarind pulp and freeze in ice-cube trays. It will keep for up to 2 months.

Serves 4

INGREDIENTS
225 g/8 oz/1¼ cups dried chick-peas
50 g/2 oz tamarind pulp
120 ml/4 fl oz/½ cup boiling water
45 ml/3 tbsp oil
2.5 ml/½ tsp cumin seeds
1 onion, finely chopped
2 garlic cloves, crushed
2.5 cm/1 in piece root ginger, grated
1 green chilli, finely chopped
5 ml/1 tsp ground cumin
5 ml/1 tsp ground coriander
1.5 ml/¼ tsp ground turmeric
2.5 ml/½ tsp salt
225 g/8 oz tomatoes, skinned and
    finely chopped
2.5 ml/½ tsp garam masala
chopped chillies and chopped
    onion, to garnish

oil
tamarind pulp
chick-peas
tomatoes
ground coriander
ground cumin
onion
cumin seeds
root ginger
ground turmeric
salt
green chilli
garam masala

1 Put the chick-peas in a large bowl and cover with plenty of cold water. Leave to soak overnight.

2 Drain the chick-peas and place in a large saucepan with double the volume of cold water. Bring to the boil and boil vigorously for 10 minutes. Skim off any scum. Cover and simmer for 1½–2 hours or until the chick-peas are soft.

3 Meanwhile, break up the tamarind and soak in the boiling water for about 15 minutes. Rub the tamarind through a sieve into a bowl, discarding any stones and fibre.

4 Heat the oil in a large saucepan and fry the cumin seeds for 2 minutes until they splutter. Add the onion, garlic, ginger and chilli and fry for 5 minutes.

5 Add the cumin, coriander, turmeric and salt and fry for 3–4 minutes. Add the tomatoes and tamarind pulp. Bring to the boil and simmer for 5 minutes.

6 Add the chick-peas and garam masala. Cover and simmer for about 15 minutes. Garnish with chopped chillies and onion.

Lentils and Rice

Lentils are cooked with whole and ground spices, potatoes, rice and onions to produce an authentic Indian-style risotto.

Serves 4

INGREDIENTS
150 g/5 oz/³⁄₄ cup toovar dhal or red
   split lentils
115 g/4 oz basmati rice
1 large potato
1 large onion
30 ml/2 tbsp oil
4 whole cloves
1.5 ml/¹⁄₄ tsp cumin seeds
1.5 ml/¹⁄₄ tsp ground turmeric
10 ml/2 tsp salt
300 ml/¹⁄₂ pints/1¹⁄₄ cups water

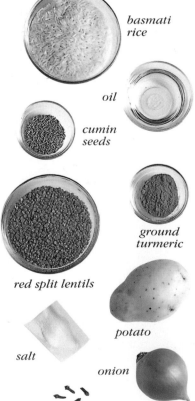

basmati rice

oil

cumin seeds

ground turmeric

red split lentils

potato

salt

onion

cloves

1 Wash the toovar dhal or lentils and rice in several changes of cold water. Put into a bowl and cover with water. Leave to soak for 15 minutes then drain.

2 Peel then cut the potato into 2.5 cm/1 in chunks.

3 Thinly slice the onion.

4 Heat the oil in a large heavy-based saucepan and fry the cloves and cumin seeds for 2 minutes until the seeds are beginning to splutter.

5 Add the onion and potatoes and fry for 5 minutes. Add the lentils, rice, turmeric and salt and fry for 3 minutes.

6 Add the water. Bring to the boil, cover and simmer for 15–20 minutes until all the water has been absorbed and the potatoes are tender. Leave to stand, covered, for about 10 minutes before serving.

Mung Beans with Potatoes

Mung beans are one of the quicker-cooking pulses which do not require soaking and are therefore very easy to use. In this recipe they are cooked with potatoes and traditional Indian spices to give a tasty nutritious dish.

Serves 4

INGREDIENTS

175 g/6 oz/1 cup mung beans
750 ml/1¼ pints/3 cups water
225 g/8 oz potatoes, cut into
    2 cm/¾ in chunks
30 ml/2 tbsp oil
2.5 ml/½ tsp cumin seeds
1 green chilli, finely chopped
1 garlic clove, crushed
2.5 cm/1 in piece root ginger,
    finely chopped
1.5 ml/¼ tsp ground turmeric
2.5 ml/½ tsp chilli powder
5 ml/1 tsp salt
5 ml/1 tsp sugar
4 curry leaves
5 tomatoes, skinned and
    finely chopped
15 ml/1 tbsp tomato purée
curry leaves, to garnish
plain rice, to serve

potatoes

mung beans

tomatoes

oil

chilli powder

tomato purée

root ginger

sugar

garlic

cumin seeds

ground turmeric

green chilli

curry leaves

salt

1 Wash the beans. Bring to the boil in the water, cover and simmer until soft, about 30 minutes. Par-boil the potatoes for 10 minutes in another saucepan, then drain well.

2 Heat the oil and fry the cumin seeds until they splutter. Add the chilli, garlic and ginger and fry for 3–4 minutes.

3 Add the turmeric, chilli powder, salt and sugar and cook for 2 minutes, stirring to prevent the mixture from sticking to the saucepan.

4 Add the curry leaves, tomatoes and tomato purée and simmer for 5 minutes until the sauce thickens. Add the tomato sauce and potatoes to the mung beans and mix together. Serve with plain boiled rice, and garnish with curry leaves.

Madras Sambal

There are many variations of this dish but it is regularly cooked in one form or another in almost every south-Indian home and served as part of a meal. You can use any combination of vegetables that are in season.

Serves 4

INGREDIENTS

225 g/8 oz/1 cup toovar dhal or red
    split lentils
600 ml/1 pint/2½ cups water
2.5 ml/½ tsp ground turmeric
2 large potatoes, cut into
    2.5 cm/1 in chunks
30 ml/2 tbsp oil
2.5 ml/½ tsp black mustard seeds
1.5 ml/¼ tsp fenugreek seeds
4 curry leaves
1 onion, thinly sliced
115 g/4 oz French beans, cut
    into 2.5 cm/1 in lengths
5 ml/1 tsp salt
2.5 ml/½ tsp chilli powder
15 ml/1 tbsp lemon juice
60 ml/4 tbsp desiccated coconut
toasted coconut, to garnish
Coriander Chutney, to serve

toovar dhal

black mustard seeds

ground turmeric

fenugreek seeds

desiccated coconut

chilli powder

potatoes

lemon juice

curry leaves

onion

French beans

1 Wash the toovar dhal or lentils in several changes of water. Place in a heavy-based saucepan with the water and the turmeric. Cover and simmer for 30–35 minutes until the lentils are soft.

2 Par-boil the potatoes in a large pan of boiling water for 10 minutes. Drain well and set aside.

3 Heat the oil in a large frying pan and fry the mustard seeds, fenugreek seeds and curry leaves for 2–3 minutes until the seeds begin to splutter. Add the onion and the French beans and fry for 7–8 minutes. Add the potatoes and cook for a further 2 minutes.

4 Stir in the the lentils with the salt, chilli powder and lemon juice and simmer for 2 minutes. Stir in the coconut and simmer for 5 minutes. Garnish with toasted coconut and serve with freshly made Coriander Chutney.

Mixed Bean Curry

You can use any combination of beans that you have in the storecupboard for this recipe.

Serves 4

INGREDIENTS

50 g/2 oz/¹/₃ cup red kidney beans
50 g/2 oz/¹/₃ cup black-eyed beans
50 g/2 oz/¹/₃ cup haricot beans
50 g/2 oz/¹/₃ cup flageolet beans
30 ml/2 tbsp oil
5 ml/1 tsp cumin seeds
5 ml/1 tsp black mustard seeds
1 onion, finely chopped
2 garlic cloves, crushed
2.5 cm/1 in piece root ginger, grated
2 green chillies, finely chopped
30 ml/2 tbsp curry paste
2.5 ml/¹/₂ tsp salt
400 g/14 oz can chopped tomatoes
30 ml/2 tbsp tomato purée
250 ml/8 fl oz/1 cup water
30 ml/2 tbsp chopped
    fresh coriander
chopped fresh coriander, to garnish

black mustard seeds
chopped tomatoes
curry paste
cumin seeds
oil
black-eyed beans
red kidney beans
tomato purée
haricot beans
onion
flageolet beans
root ginger
green chillies
fresh coriander
garlic

1 Put the beans in a large bowl and cover with plenty of cold water. Leave to soak overnight, mixing occasionally.

2 Drain the beans and put into a large heavy-based saucepan with double the volume of cold water. Boil vigorously for 10 minutes. Skim off any scum. Cover and simmer for 1¹/₂ hours or until the beans are soft.

3 Heat the oil in a large saucepan and fry the cumin seeds and mustard seeds for 2 minutes until the seeds begin to splutter. Add the onion, garlic, ginger and chilli and fry for 5 minutes.

4 Add the curry paste and fry for a further 2–3 minutes, stirring, then add the salt.

5 Add the tomatoes, tomato purée and the water and simmer for 5 minutes.

6 Add the drained beans and the fresh coriander. Cover and simmer for about 30–40 minutes until the sauce thickens and the beans are cooked. Garnish with chopped fresh coriander.

COOK'S TIP
Depending on the types of beans you use, you may need to adjust the cooking time.

Egg and Lentil Curry

A few Indian spices can transform eggs and lentils into a tasty, economical curry.

Serves 4

INGREDIENTS

75 g/3 oz green lentils
750 ml/1¼ pints/3 cups
    vegetable stock
6 eggs
30 ml/2 tbsp oil
3 cloves
1.5 ml/¼ tsp black peppercorns
1 onion, finely chopped
2 green chillies, finely chopped
2 garlic cloves, crushed
2.5 cm/1 in root ginger,
    finely chopped
30 ml/2 tbsp curry paste
400 g/14 oz can chopped tomatoes
2.5 ml/½ tsp sugar
2.5 ml/½ tsp garam masala

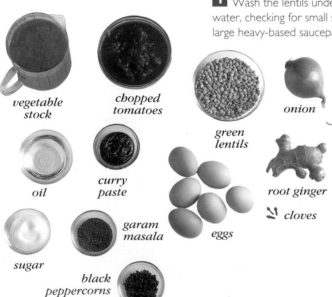

vegetable stock

chopped tomatoes

oil

curry paste

green lentils

onion

root ginger

cloves

green chilli

garlic

eggs

sugar

garam masala

black peppercorns

1 Wash the lentils under cold running water, checking for small stones. Put in a large heavy-based saucepan with the stock. Cover and simmer gently for about 15 minutes or until the lentils are soft. Drain and set aside.

2 Cook the eggs in boiling water for 10 minutes. When cool enough to handle, peel and cut in half lengthways.

3 Heat the oil in a large saucepan and fry the cloves and peppercorns for about 2 minutes. Add the onion, chillies, garlic and ginger and fry the mixture for a further 5–6 minutes.

4 Stir in the curry paste and fry for 2 minutes.

5 Stir in the tomatoes and sugar with 175 ml/6 fl oz/³/₄ cup water.

6 Simmer for 5 minutes until the sauce thickens. Add the eggs, drained lentils and garam masala. Cover and simmer for about 10 minutes, then serve.

Vegetable Pilau

A popular vegetable rice dish that goes well with most Indian meat dishes.

Serves 4–6

INGREDIENTS
225 g/8 oz/1 cup basmati rice
30 ml/2 tbsp oil
2.5 ml/½ tsp cumin seeds
2 bay leaves
4 green cardamom pods
4 cloves
1 onion, finely chopped
1 carrot, finely diced
50 g/2 oz/½ cup frozen
  peas, thawed
50 g/2 oz/⅓ cup frozen sweetcorn,
thawed
25 g/1 oz/¼ cup cashew nuts,
  lightly fried
475 ml/16 fl oz/2 cups water
1.5 ml/¼ tsp ground cumin

basmati rice

peas

ground
coriander

cumin seeds

carrot

sweetcorn

ground
cumin

bay
leaves

oil

onion

cashew
nuts

cardamom
pods

cloves

salt

1 Wash the basmati rice in several changes of cold water. Put into a bowl and cover with water. Leave to soak for 30 minutes.

2 Heat the oil in a large frying pan and fry the cumin seeds for 2 minutes. Add the bay leaves, cardamoms and cloves and fry for 2 minutes.

3 Add the onion and fry for 5 minutes until lightly browned.

4 Stir in the carrot and cook for 3–4 minutes.

5 Drain the rice and add to the pan with the peas, sweetcorn and cashew nuts. Fry for 4–5 minutes.

6 Add the water, remaining spices and salt. Bring to the boil, cover, and simmer for 15 minutes over a low heat until all the water is absorbed. Leave to stand, covered, for 10 minutes before serving.